Distributed Multiple Description Coding

Huihui Bai • Anhong Wang • Yao Zhao
Jeng-Shyang Pan • Ajith Abraham

Distributed Multiple Description Coding

Principles, Algorithms and Systems

Dr. Huihui Bai
Institute of Information Science
Beijing Jiaotong University
Beijing 100044
China, People's Republic
luckybhh@gmail.com

Prof. Yao Zhao
Institute of Information Science
Beijing Jiaotong University
Beijing 100044
China, People's Republic
yzhao@bjtu.edu.cn

Prof. (Dr.) Ajith Abraham
Director – Machine Intelligence Research
Labs (MIR Labs)
Scientific Network for Innovation
and Research Excellence
P.O. Box 2259 Auburn, Washington 98071,
USA
ajith.abraham@ieee.org

Prof. Anhong Wang
Taiyuan University of Science
and Technology
Taiyuan 030024
China, People's Republic
wah_ty@yahoo.com.cn

Prof. Jeng-Shyang Pan
Department of Electronic Engineering
Nat. Kaohsiung University of Applied
Sciences
Chien-Kung Road 415
80778 Kaohsiung
Taiwan R.O.C.
jspan@cc.kuas.edu.tw

ISBN 978-1-4471-2247-0   e-ISBN 978-1-4471-2248-7
DOI 10.1007/978-1-4471-2248-7
Springer London Dordrecht Heidelberg New York

British Library Cataloguing in Publication Data
A catalogue record for this book is available from the British Library

Library of Congress Control Number: 2011940972

Springer is part of Springer Science+Business Media (www.springer.com)

Preface

In the past decade or so, there have been fascinating developments in image and video compression. The establishment of many international standards by ISO/MPEG and ITU-T laid the common groundwork for different vendors and content providers. The explosive growth of the network, multimedia, and wireless is fundamentally changing the way people communicate with each other. Real-time reliable transmission of image and video has become an inevitable demand. As we all know, due to bandwidth and time limitation, highly efficient compression must be applied to the original data. However, lower ability of wireless terminals, network congestion, as well as network heterogeneity have posed great challenges on the conventional image and video compression coding.

To address the problems, two novel techniques, distributed video coding (DVC) and multiple description coding (MDC), are illustrated in this book. DVC can effectively reduce the complexity of conventional encoders, so as to meet the lower capacity of wireless terminals, and MDC can realize the reliable transmission over error-prone channels.

This book is dedicated for addressing the DVC and MDC issues in a systematic way. After giving a state-of-the-art survey, we propose some novel DVC and MDC improvements for image and video transmission, with an attempt to achieve better performance. For each DVC and MDC approach, the main idea and corresponding algorithms design are elaborated in detail.

This book covers the fundamental concepts and the core technologies of DVC and MDC, especially its latest developments. Each chapter is presented in a self-sufficient and independent way so that the reader can select the chapters interesting to them. The methodologies are described in detail so that the readers can repeat the corresponding experiments easily.

For researchers, it would be a good book for inspiring new ideas about the novel DVC and MDC technologies, and a quick way to learn new ideas from the current status of DVC and MDC. For engineers, it would be a good guidebook to develop practical applications for DVC and MDC system.

Chapter 1 provides a broad overview of DVC and MDC, from basic ideas to the current research. Chapter 2 focuses on the principles of MDC, such as sub-sampling based MDC, quantization based MDC, transform based MDC, and FEC based MDC. Chapter 3 presents the principles of DVC, mainly including Slepian-Wolf coding based on Turbo and LDPC respectively and comparing the relative performance. Chapters 4 and 5 are devoted to the algorithms of MDC and DVC, mainly focusing on the current research fruits of the authors. We provide the basic frameworks and the experimental results, which may help the readers improve the efficiency of MDC and DVC. Chapter 6 introduces the classical DVC system for mobile communications, providing the developmental environment in detail.

This work was supported in part by Sino-Singapore JRP (No. 2010DFA11010), National Natural Science Foundation of China (No. 61073142, No. 60903066, No. 60972085), Beijing Natural Science Foundation (No. 4102049), Specialized Research Fund for the Doctoral Program of Higher Education (No. 20090009120006), Doctor Startup Foundation of TYUST (20092011), International Cooperative Program of Shanxi Province (No. 2011081055) and The Shanxi Provincial Foundation for Leaders of Disciplines in Science (No. 20111022).

We are very much grateful to the Springer in-house editors, Simon Rees (Associate Editor) and Wayne Wheeler (Senior Editor), for the editorial assistance and excellent cooperative collaboration to produce this important scientific work. We hope that the reader will share our excitement to present this book and will find it useful.

Huihui Bai
Anhong Wang
Yao Zhao
Jeng-Shyang Pan
Ajith Abraham

Contents

Chapter 1
Introduction

1.1 Background

In home theater, VCD, DVD, and other multimedia applications and visual communications such as video phone and video conference, how to effectively reduce the amount of data and the occupied frequency band is an important issue necessary to be solved. Among these application cases, image and video occupy the most amounts of data; therefore, how to use as little data as possible to represent the image and video without distortion has become the key to these applications, which is the main issue of image and video compression.

Research on image compression has been done during the last several years. Researchers have proposed various compression methods such as DPCM, DCT, VQ, ISO/IEC, and ITU-T, and other international organizations have made many successful image and video standards [1–8], such as the still image video standard represented by JPEG and JPEG-2000, the coding standard of high-rate multimedia data represented by MPEG-1 and MPEG-2 whose main content is video image compression standard, the moving image compression standard of low bit rate, very low bit rate represented by H.261, H.263, H.263+, H.263++, H.264/AVC, as well as the MPEG-4 standard of object-oriented applications.

In recent years, with the popularization and promotion of the Internet and personal radio communication equipments, it has become an inevitable demand to transmit image and video at real time in packet-switching networks and narrowband networks. Meanwhile, the low computing power of wireless multimedia terminal equipment and the increasingly serious congestion problem in wireless communication networks and the Internet, along with the growing complexity of heterogeneity in networks, have brought great challenges to the traditional video image coding.

From the perspective of the network device context, on the one hand, current network communication involves a large number of mobile video intake equipments, such as mobile camera phones, large-scale sensor network, video monitoring on network, and so on. All these equipments possess the intake functions of

H. Bai et al., *Distributed Multiple Description Coding*,
DOI 10.1007/978-1-4471-2248-7_1, © Springer-Verlag London Limited 2011

image and video, which are needed to conduct on-site video coding and transmit the stream into center node, decoding, and playing. These devices are relatively simple, and the operational ability and power itself is very limited. There exist significant differences between the aspects of power display processing capabilities and memory support hardware and traditional computing equipments that are far from being able to meet the high complexity of motion estimation and other algorithms in traditional video coding, but in the decoding end (such as base stations, center nodes) have more computing resources and are able to conduct complex calculations, contrary to application occasions of the traditional video coding. On the other hand, there exist problems of channel interference, network congestion, and routing delay in the Internet network that will lead to data error and packet loss, while the random bit error and unexpected error and other problems in wireless communication network channel further worsen the channel status, making for a large number of fields of transmitted video data failure or loss. These problems are fatal to data compression because the compressed data are generally the stream consisting of unequally long codes, which will cause error diffusion and other issues. If there is an error or data packet loss, this will not only affect the service quality of video business but also cause the entire video communication system to completely fail and become the bottleneck of restrictions on the development of real-time network video technology.

From the perspective of video coding, the traditional video coding method, such as MPEG, H.26X series standard, as a result of using motion estimation, motion compensation, orthogonal transformation, scalar quantization, and entropy coding in the coding end, causes higher computational complexity. Motion estimation is the principle mean to remove the correlation between the video frames, but at the same time, it is a most complex operation, because every coding block must do similarity calculations with every block of the reference picture. Comparatively speaking, in the decoding end, without the search operation of motion estimation, its complexity is five to ten times easier than the coding end. Therefore, the traditional video coding method is applied in situations when the coding end has stronger computational capabilities or the one-time compression and multiple decoding of non-real time, such as broadcasting, streaming media VOD services, and so on. On the other hand, the traditional video coding focused more upon improving the compressive properties, when data transformation error occurred, is mainly dependent on the correcting capacity of post-channel coding. The international video coding standard set recently, such as the Fine Granularity Scalability in MPEG-4 [9] and the Progressive Fine Granularity Scalability with higher quality proposed by Wu Feng [10], also tries to adopt a new coding frame to better adapt to the network transmission. In FGS coding, in order to ensure the reliability of transmission, the basic layer adopts stronger error protection measures such as the stronger FEC and ARQ. But the following problems exist in this method: firstly, the system quality will seriously decline when the network packet loss is serious; in addition, repeat ARQ will cause excessive delay; and strong FEC will also bring additional delay because of its complexity, seriously affecting the real-time play of the video.

All in all, in order to provide high-quality video services to the users in wireless mobile terminals, we must overcome the low operational ability in the terminal and the problem caused by unreliable transmission in the existing network; therefore, we should design video coding which has low coding complexity and strong error-resilient ability.

1.2 Multiple Description Coding (MDC)

1.2.1 Basic Idea of MDC

The basic idea of multiple description coding (MDC) is to encode the source into many descriptions (bit stream) of equal importance and transfer them on non-priority and unreliable networks. At the receiving end, receiving any description can restore rough but acceptable approximation compared to the original coded image. With the increasing number of the received descriptions, the precision of reconstructed quality will gradually improve, thus, effectively solving the problem of serious decline in quality when the traditional source encoding encounters packet loss and delay on unreliable network.

Each description generated by the multiple description coding has the following characteristics: Firstly, the importance of each description is the same and does not need to design network priority specially, thus reducing the cost and complexity of the network design. Secondly, every description being independent, the decoder end can decode independently when receiving any description and reconstruct the sources with acceptable quality. Thirdly, all descriptions have dependency, that is, apart from the important information of one's own, every description also includes redundant information that helps to restore other descriptions. Therefore, the results of decoding reconstruction will improve with the increasing number of received descriptions. If every description can be received accurately, we can get high-quality reconstruction signals in the decoder end [11].

The most typical multiple description encoder model encodes a source into two descriptions, S_1 and S_2, and transmits in two separate channels. As Fig. 1.1 illustrates, an MDC model possesses two channels and three decoders. In the decoder end, if we only receive the description of channel 1 or channel 2, then we can get the acceptable single road reconstruction through the corresponding single channel decoder 1 or 2. The distortion caused by this is recorded as single channel distortion D_1 or D_2; if the descriptions of two channels can be received accurately, then through the center of the decoder, we can get reconstruction of high quality. The distortion caused by the two-way reconstruction is called center distortion, known as D_0. The rate of transmission in channel 1 or channel 2 is the required bit number for each pixel of source.

Figure 1.2 shows the comparison of nonprogressive and progressive coding and multiple description coding under retransmission mechanism. In the three cases, the images are all transmitted by the six packets, but in the process of transfer, the

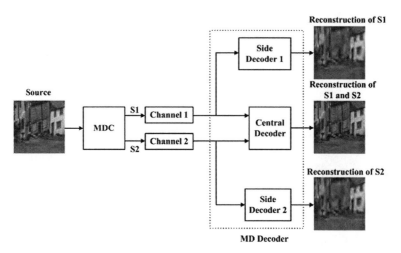

Fig. 1.1 MDC model with two channels and three decoders

third packet is lost. As evident, when receiving the first two packets, nonprogressive coding can only restore some of the image information, progressive coding and multiple description coding can restore comparative fuzzy image information, and the reconstruction effect of progressive coding is better than multiple description coding. When the third data packet is lost, the image quality of nonprogressive coding and progressive coding comes to a standstill, the main reason being that these two schemes must base on the former data packet to decode the present one; therefore, the data packets we receive after the loss of the third one have no effect. We must wait for the successfully retransmission of the third one; however, the retransmission time is usually longer than the interval of data packets, thus causing unnecessary delay. However, using multiple description coding technology is not affected by the loss of the third packet at all; the image quality is constantly improving as the packets arrive one by one. From the time when the packet is lost to its successful retransmit, the image quality of multiple description coding is undoubtedly the best. Thus, it can be seen that when packet loss occurs, we can use multiple description coding to transfer acceptable image for users faster.

We can see that multiple description coding is mainly used for loss compression and transmission of signals; that is, data may be lost during the transfer process. The restored signals allow a certain degree of distortion, for example, the compressing and transfer of image, audio, video, and other signals. The occasions for application are mainly as follows.

1.2.1.1   Internet Communication

Since the MDC has the characteristic of transfer on unreliable signal channel, it has a wide application in the case of packet-switching networks. The Internet is

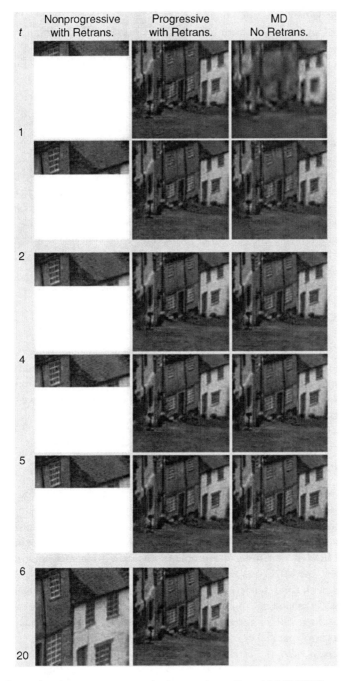

Fig. 1.2 Comparison between nonprogressive/progressive coding with MDC [11]

usually affected by network congestion, backbone network capacity, bandwidth, and route selecting, which result in loss of data packets. The traditional solution is ARQ; however, this method needs feedback mechanism and will further aggravate congestion and delay, so it is not conducive to the application of real-time demand. In addition, the existing layered coding requires the network to have priority and have the ability to treat the data packets differently, thus increasing the complexity of network design. But using MDC helps avoid these situations.

1.2.1.2   Partition Storage System

As for large image databases, adopt MDC to copy and store the image in different positions, so that when fast browsing, we can quickly find a copy of low quality stored in the nearest region; if we need an image of higher quality, we can search one or several image copies stored in further areas and combine it with the copy of the nearest area to improve the reconstruct quality of the image, and thus meet the needs of various applications.

1.2.1.3   Wireless Communication

Because of channel fading, wireless communication often causes longer unexpected bit error; the solution is to divide the signal channel into several virtual ones, such as frequency hopping system is quite fit for MDC technology. In addition, the MDC technology is also effective in solving the adjacent channel interference problem of the wireless broadcasting system.

1.2.2   Review of Multiple Description Coding

The history of MDC can be traced back to the 1970s, when Bell Laboratories carried out odd and even separation of the signal from the same call and transferred it in two separate channels in order to provide continuous telephone service in telephone networks [12]. At that time, the problem was called channel splitting by Bell Laboratories. The MDC was formally put forward in September 1979, on Shannon Theory Research Conference, at which time Gersho, Ozarow, Witsenhausen, Wolf, Wyner, and Ziv made the following issues: if a source is described by two separate descriptions, how will the reconstruct quality of signal source be affected when the descriptions are separated or combined? The problem is called multiple description problem. In this field, the original basic theory was put forward by the abovementioned researchers and Ahlswede, Berger, Cover, Gamal, and Zhang in the 1980s. Earlier studies mainly focused on five elements function $(R_1, R_2, D_0, D_1, D_2)$ produced by MDC, which has two channels and three decoders. At the conference on Shannon theory research in September 1979, Wyner, Witsenhausen, Wolf, and

Ziv gave the preliminary conclusions of MDC when dual source under the Hamming distortion. For any zero memory information source and the given distortion vector under bounded distortion (D_0, D_1, D_2), Gamal and Cover gave the reachable rate area (R_1, R_2) [13]. Ozarow proved that the above areas were tight to non-memory Gaussian source and square error [14]. Then Ahlswede pointed out that when there is no residual rate, that is, $R_1 + R_2 = R(D_0)$, the above Gamal-Cover limit was tight [15]. Zhang and Bergner proved that if $D_0 > D(R_1 + R_2)$, the above boundaries were not tight [16]. The above conclusions were studied on Gaussian information source, yet we do not fully know the rate-distortion boundaries of non-Gaussian information sources. Zimir studied on MDC under mean square error of non-discrete and zero memory information sources. Given the scope of rate distortion, in fact, it is the extension of Shannon boundary under rate-distortion function [17]. As to the research on the reachable region of five elements function $(R_1, R_2, D_0, D_1, D_2)$, the main task was concentrated on non-memory binary symmetric source under Hamming distortion.

In the early stage, the MDC mainly conducted theoretical studies. After Vaishampayan gave the first practical MDC method, multiple description scalar quantization [18], research on MDC changed from theoretical investigation to the construction of practical MDC system. Around 1998, MDC became the research hotspot for many scholars; many new MDC methods emerged, such as the MDC based on subsampling, MDC based on quantization, transform-based MDC, and so on. In Chapter 2 we will introduce these in detail.

The national multiple description video coding began in 1990. Some of the existing MDC are encoding schemes of block-based motion estimation and motion compensation; this will inevitably involve the problem of mismatch correction, that is, how to deal with the problem of inconsistent frame in codec caused by signal channel error [19]. In addition, MDC must consider the issue of non-real multiple description signal channel. Some existing MDC methods were put forward in the hypothesis of the ideal multiple description signal channel; the descriptions transmitted in an ideal signal channel can be all received correctly or lost. But in fact, both the Internet and the wireless channel are not ideal description channels; the packet may be lost randomly in any channel. Therefore, the multiple description video coding scheme should also consider the effect of multiple description channel to the video reconstruct quality.

1.3 Distributed Video Coding (DVC)

1.3.1 Basic Idea of DVC

In order to solve the problem of high complexity in traditional video coding, Distributed Source Coding (DSC) gets attention of more and more scholars. DSC bases on the theory of source coding in the 1970s: theory of Slepian–Wolf

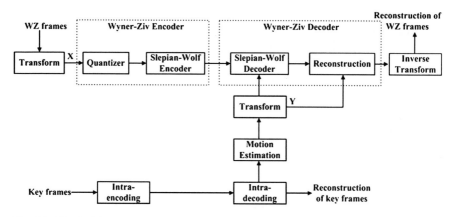

Fig. 1.3 Classical framework of DVC

[20, 21] under lossless circumstance and theory of Wyner–Ziv [22–24] under distortion circumstance, including the following Wyner–Ziv coding theory of decoding side information [25, 26]; these theories abandon the traditional principle that only the coding end can use the statistical characteristic of signal sources and propose that we can also achieve effective compression in the decoding end by using the statistical characteristic of signal.

Distributed Video Coding (DVC) [27] is the successful application of DSC theory in video compression; its basic idea is regarding the adjacent frames of the video as related source and adopting the coding frame of "independent coding and joint decoding" for adjacent frames, which has essential difference with the structure of "joint coding and joint decoding" for adjacent frames in traditional video coding standard MPEG. The typical DVC, as shown in Fig. 1.3, extracts a group of frames with equal interval from the image sequence to code which are called key frames; its coding and decoding adopt the traditional intra ways, such as H.264 coding technology. The frames between the key frames are called WZ frames; these frames adopt the coding method of intra coding and inter decoding. Because WZ coding transfers some or all of the motion estimation of huge amount of calculation in traditional video coding algorithm to the decoding end, DVC realizes low-complexity encoding. In addition, in WZ encoder, the Slepian–Wolf encoder is created by channel codes, and its decoding end adopts error-correcting algorithm of channel codes. When the error-correcting ability of channel code is strong, even if error occurs during the transmission of WZ code stream, it can be corrected. Therefore, DVC has a certain robustness of channel transmission, which is because of low-complexity coding. DVC is particularly suitable for the transmission requirement of the emerging low power consumption network terminal.

Figure 1.4 illustrates an example of the application of DVC in the low power consumption mobile phone communication which adopts the method of transcoding to realize video communication between two mobile phones with low operational ability. Take the communication from A to B as an example – A is compressed

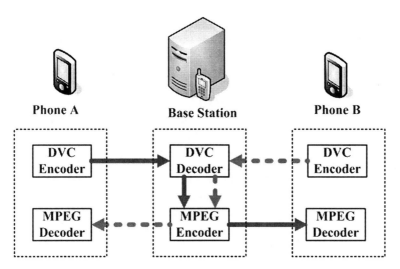

Fig. 1.4 Transcoding architecture for wireless video

by the DVC method of low complexity coding – then transmit the compressed bit stream to mobile network base station which can change the distributed video stream into MPEG stream and then transfer the stream to mobile phone B; it can get the restored video by using MPEG decoding algorithm of lower complexity. This kind of communication mode integrates the advantage of coding method of DVC and traditional MPEG; the mobile terminal only needs simple calculation, and a large number of calculations focus on a specific device in network, thus satisfying the "'low-complexity encoding' demand of low energy consumption devices."

However, DVC as a new coding framework different from traditional encoding, there is still much room for improvements such as compressive properties, robustness of adapting to network transmission, and scalability, etc.; the following sections will analyze its research status and disadvantages from various aspects.

1.3.2 Review of DVC

Analyzing the coding framework of Fig. 1.3 again, generally speaking, WZ encoder consists of quantizer and a Slepain–Wolf encoder based on channel code, for X – the input of WZ (also called main information), DVC can be divided into two schemes – pixel domain and transform domain; the former directly uses WZ encoding for the pixel of WZ frame, while the latter first transforms WZ frame and then compresses the transform coefficients by WZ encoder. Girod of Stanford University in the USA realized the DVC in pixel domain earlier [28–30], adopted uniform scalar quantization for every pixel, and compressed the quantized sequence by Slepian–Wolf encoder based on Turbo code. WZ encoding in the pixel domain has obtained the rate distortion performance between the traditional intra coding and inter coding, and then the Girod task group applied the DCT transformation into DVC and proposed DVC in DCT domain based on Turbo code [31, 32]. Ramchandran [33–35] also proposed the scheme of DVC in DCT domain, that is, the scheme of power-efficient, robust, high compression, and syndrome-based multimedia coding; they do scalar quantization for DCT transform coefficients of 8×8 and compress the quantized DCT coefficients by trellis code. Because transform coding further removed the space redundancy of the image, the effect of DVC in DCT domain is better than that in pixel domain. On the basis of the above proposed scheme, someone proposed some improved algorithm to develop the performance of DVC, such as PRISM in wavelet domain [36], a series of algorithms based on Girod framework proposed by the organization DISCOVER in Europe [37, 38].

However, the current research results show that the performance of DVC is between the traditional intra coding and inter coding; it still has a large gap compared with the traditional intra video coding standard and, therefore, how to improve the compressive properties of DVC is one of the current research topics, followed by analysis according to the various modules of DVC framework.

First of all, in the aspects of quantization module design, the quantizer in WZ encoder conducts certain compression for the signal source and at the same time represents the signal source as an index sequence to facilitate the decoding end to do index resumed by using side information. For easy implementation, almost every DVC adopts uniform scalar quantization; for example, the DVC in pixel domain applies SQ directly into various pixels, DVC in DCT domain applies the scalar quantization into DCT coefficients, etc., but the performance of simple scalar quantization is not satisfying. Some documents do theory and application research on the quantizer in WZ encoding. Zamir and Shamai proved that when the signal-to-noise is high, when the main information and side information are joint Gaussian source, then the nested liner lattice quantization can approach WZ rate distortion function, so [39, 40] made the enlightenment design scheme while Xiong et al. [41] and Liu et al. [42] proposed a nested lattice quantization and Slepian–Wolf encoder, then applied the scheme of the combination of trellis [43] and lattice. On the issue of DSC quantizer optimization, Fleming et al. [44] consider using Lloyd algorithm [45] to get the locally optimal WZ vector quantization to realize the optimization of fixed rate. Fleming and Effros [46] adopted the rate-distortion optimized vector quantization, regarding the bit rate as quantization index function, but the efficiency of the scheme is low and complex. Muresan and Effros [47] implemented the problem of looking for local optimum quantization from the adjacent regions. In [48] they illustrated the scheme of [47] and restricted its global optimization due to the adjacent codeword. In [49], authors considered applying the Lloyd to Slepian–Wolf encoding without side information. The Girod task group applied the method of Lloyd into the general ideal Slepian–Wolf encoder whose bit rate depends on the index and side information of the quantizer; Rebollo-Monedero et al. [50] illustrated that when the bit rate is high, and under certain constraints, the most optimized quantizer is lattice quantizer, and also verified the experimental results of [51]. In addition, Tang et al. [52] proposed the application of wavelet transform and embedded SPIHT quantization method into multispectral image compression.

In short, the pursuit of simple, practical, and optimized transform and quantification method is a key to improve the performance of DVC.

Secondly, in terms of Slepian–Wolf encoder module, many researchers put forward a number of improved methods. Slepian–Wolf encoder is another key technology of DVC. Although the theories in 1970s have indicated that Slepian–Wolf encoding and channel coding are closely related, in recent years the emergence of high-performance channel code, such as Turbo code and LDPC code, has led to the gradual appearance of some practical Slepian–Wolf encoders. In 1999, Pradhan and Ramchandran proposed the use of the trellis [39, 53–56] as Slepian–Wolf encoder, later Wang and Orchard [57] proposed the embedded trellis Slepian–Wolf encoder; since then, channel coding technology of higher performance was applied to DSC, such as the compression scheme based on Turbo code [58–65]. Later research found that the Slepian–Wolf based on low density parity check is closer to the ideal limit. Schonberg et al., Leveris et al., and Varodayan et al. [66–68] compressed the binary sources by LDPC encoder, and from then on, it raised people's research interest and widespread attention. The difference between the bit rate of Slepian–Wolf encoder and the ideal Slepian–Wolf limit reflects the quality of its performance; the distance between the most common Turbo code Slepian–Wolf encoder and the ideal limit is 3–11% [59], while the distance between the LDPC-based Slepian–Wolf encoder and ideal limit is still 5–10% [68]. The gap is large when the correlation between primary information and side information is low and the code length is short; therefore, pursuing a higher compression rate while reducing the gap with Slepian–Wolf limit is a research goal of Slepian–Wolf encoder for a long time.

In addition, the realization of bit rate adaptive control is also a key issue for the practical of Slepian–Wolf encoder; the effect of Slepian–Wolf encoder to DVC is similar to that of entropy encoding to traditional coding, but in traditional coding, because the coding end knows the statistical correlation of the source, it can send bits correctly according to the correlation and achieve lossless recovery. However, in DVC, because the coding end does not know the correlation of the side information, it cannot know the number of the required bits for lossless recovery of the decoding end, causing the blind rate control. At present, we often use decoding end and feedback channel to achieve rate adaptive of DVC, such as the Girod scheme and so on, but feedback brings about limitations to practical application. The scheme of PRISM proposed that conducting simple estimation for time correlation in the coding end to send the syndrome, although the proposal does not use the feedback, leads to the incorrectness of the syndrome bit due to the gap of correlation between the coding end and decoding end. The later documents research on the problem of how to remove the feedback channel; for example, Brites and Pereira [69] suggest that by using the bit rate control in the coding end to remove feedback, the rate distortion performance reduces about 1.2 dB compared with that of using bit rate control in the decoding end. Tonomura et al. [70] proposed using the cross-probability of bit plane to estimate the check bit to be sent by DVC and thus remove the feedback channel. Bernardini et al. [71] put forward use of the fold function to process the wavelet coefficients, take advantage of the periodicity of the fold function, the correlation of side information, to remove the feedback. Further, Bernadini, Vitali et al. [72] use a Laplacian model to estimate the cross-probability of primary information and side information after quantization, then according to the cross-probability, send suitable WZ bit to remove the feedback channel. Moreby et al. [73] put forward the no-feedback DVC scheme in pixel domain. Yaacoub et al. [74] put forward the problem of adaptive bit allocation and variable parameters quantization in multisensor DVC and according to the motion status of video and the actual channel statistical characteristic to allocate rate.

The motion estimation in the coding end is an important factor for the success of traditional video coding; in contrast, the existing DVC scheme moves the motion estimation to the decoding end and uses the recovery frame in the decoding end to motion estimate to produce side information. However, incorrect recovery frame leads to incorrect motion estimation. This will cause the decrease in performance of side information and eventually cause the decline in DVC performance; so improving the performance of motion estimation is a critical part to improve DVC performance. Motion estimation in DVC is first proposed by the group PRISM [33–35]; they conduct cyclic redundancy check for the DCT block and send it to the receiver by comparing the reference block and the present block of side information to assist motion estimation, but the scheme is relatively complex. Girod of Stanford [28–31] first used the motion estimation interpolation to produce side information, but the performance of this method is lower because it does not use any information of the current frame. In order to maintain the simple properties of the encoder and to obtain the information of the current frame, in Aaron et al. [75]. Girod puts forward a Hash-based motion estimation method; that is, the coding end adopts a subset of the DCT quantization coefficients as the Hash and sends it to the decoding end, based on the received Hash information, and conducts motion estimation in the reference block of the decoding frame to get better side information. In fact, the CRC of PRISM scheme also can be regarded as a kind of Hash information. On the basis of Girod, Ascenso and Pereira [76] put forward the adaptive Hash; Martinian et al. [77] and Wang et al. [78] put forward a low-quality reference Hash; that is, the version of WZ frame is compressed by zero motion vector H.264. However, further study is needed on the rate of Hash information, complexity, and its effectiveness on motion estimation performance. Adikari et al. [79] put forward the generating method of multiside information in the decoding end, but the complexity increased. In addition, some papers suggest that the decoding end and coding end share the motion estimation to improve the performance; for example, Sun and Tsai [80] used optical flow estimation to get the motion status of the block in the encoding end; the decoding end chose suitable generating method of side information based on this status, but to a certain degree, these methods increased the complexity of the encoding end.

Additionally, Ascenso et al. [37] put forward the gradually refined method for side information in the decoding end; it does not need the extra Hash bit and uses the information of the current frame which has been partially decoded to update the side information gradually, so it is also a good way to improve code performance. It is encouraging that Dempster et al. [81] used Expectation

Maximization to study the parallax of the current frame and other frames and formed the so-called parallax unsupervised learning [82], and it provided a very good idea for the improvement of side information performance. Some research works [83–85] applied the unsupervised method for distributed multi-view video coding and achieved very good results. In 2008, they applied this method for the generation of side information in single viewpoint DVC [86], and the experimental results show that the motion estimation in the decoding end based on EM provided very good results and improved the performance of side information. The performance of DVC improves with the increase of GOP, as per earlier studies, due to the poor performance of side information, when the GOP is larger; the performance of DVC becomes poor instead. Later, Chen et al. [87] applied the parallax-unsupervised method and Gray coding and other technologies into the research of multi-view DVC and achieved obvious effects.

In addition, the reference model of primary information and side information in DSC and DVC affects the performance of Slepian–Wolf encoder to a great extent. Bassi et al. [88] defined two practical relevance models as for Gaussian source. Brites and Pereira [89] proposed different correlation models for primary information and side information of different transform domains and put forward dynamic on-line noise model to improve the correlation estimation. The representation of the quantized primary information and side information will also affect the performance of DVC to a great extent. Gray code can represent the value with smaller Euclidean distance with smaller Hamming distance, so as to improve the correlation of quantitative binary sequences, and ultimately improve the compression rate of the Slepian–Wolf encoder. He et al. [90] proved the effectiveness of Gray code in DVC with theory and experiments, and Hua and Chen [91] proposed using Gray code, Zero-Skip, and the symbol of the coded DCT coefficients to effectively represent the correlation and eventually improve the performance.

Finally, for the quantitative reconstruction of DVC, many papers use the conditional expectation of quantified sequences in the given side information to carry out reconstruction. Weerakkody et al. [92] refined the reconstruct function, especially when the side information and the decoded quantitative value are not in the same interval; we use training and regression method to get the regression line between the bit error rate and reconstruct value, so as to improve the performance of reconstruction.

References

1. JPEG Standard, JPEG ISO/IEC 10918–1 ITU-T Recommendation T.81
2. JPEG 2000 Image coding system, ISO/IEC International standard 15444–1, ITU Recommendation T.800 (2000)
3. ISO/IEC. JCT1/SC29 CD11172–2 MPEG1. International standard for coding of moving pictures and associated audio for digital storage media at up to 1.5 Mbps (1991)
4. ISO/IEC. JCT1/SC29 CD13818–2 MPEG2. Coding of moving pictures and associated audio for digital storage (1993)

5. ISO/IEC. JCT1/SC29 WG11/N3536 MPEG4. Overview V.15 (2000)
6. ITU-T Draft ITU-T Recommendation H.261: Video codec for audio/visual communications at p × 64 kbps (1993)
7. ITU-T Draft ITU-T Recommendation H.263 (V1, V2, V3): Video coding for low bit rate communications (1996–2000)
8. JVT & ITU-T VCEG, Draft ITU-T Recommendation and final draft international standard of joint video specification H.264 (MPEG-4 Part10)[S] (7–14 Mar 2003)
9. Radha, H.M., Schaar, M.V.D., Chen, Y.: The MPEG-4 fine-grained scalable video coding method for multimedia stream over IP. IEEE Trans. Multimed. 3(3), 53–68 (2001)
10. Wu, F., Li, S., Zhang, Y.Q.: A framework for efficient progressive fine granularity scalable video coding. IEEE Trans. Circuits Syst. Video Technol. 11(3), 332–344 (2001)
11. Goyal, V.K.: Multiple description coding: compression meets the network. IEEE Signal Proc. Mag. 18(5), 74–93 (2001)
12. Jayant, N.S.: Subsampling of a DPCM speech channel to provide two 'self-contained' half-rate channels. Bell Syst. Tech. J. 60(4), 501–509 (1981)
13. El Gamal, A.A., Cover, T.M.: Achievable rates for multiple descriptions. IEEE Trans. Inf. Theory 28, 851–857 (1982)
14. Ozarow, L.: On a source-coding problem with two channels and three receivers. Bell Syst. Tech. J. 59(10), 1909–1921 (1980)
15. Ahlswede, R.: The rate distortion region for multiple description without excess rate. IEEE Trans. Inf. Theory 36(6), 721–726 (1985)
16. Lam, W. M., Reibman, A. R., Liu, B.: Recovery of lost or erroneously received motion vectors. In: IEEE International Conference on Acoustics, Speech and Signal Processing, (ICASSP'93), Minneapolis, vol. 5, pp. 417–420 (Apr 1993)
17. Zamir, R.: Gaussian codes and Shannon bounds for multiple descriptions. IEEE Trans. Inf. Theory 45, 2629–2635 (1999)
18. Vaishanmpayan, V.A.: Design of multiple description scalar quantizers. IEEE Trans. Inf. Theory 39(3), 821–834 (1993)
19. Wang, Y., Reibman, A.R., Lin, S.: Multiple description coding for video delivery. Proc. IEEE 93(1), 57–70 (2005)
20. Slepian, D., Wolf, J.K.: Noiseless coding of correlated information sources. IEEE Trans. Inf. Theory 19(4), 471–480 (1973)
21. Wyner, A.D.: Recent results in the Shanno theory. IEEE Trans. Inf. Theory 20(1), 2–10 (1974)
22. Wyner, A., Ziv, J.: The rate-distortion function for source coding with side information at the decoder. IEEE Trans. Inf. Theory 22(1), 1–10 (1976)
23. Wyner, A.D.: The rate-distortion function for source coding with side information at the decoder-II: general source. Inf. Control 38(1), 60–80 (1978)
24. Wyner, A.: On source coding with side information at the decoder. IEEE Trans. Inf. Theory 21(3), 294–300 (1975)
25. Zamir, R.: The rate loss in the Wyner-Ziv problem. IEEE Trans. Inf. Theory 42(6), 2073–2084 (1996)
26. Zamir, R., Shamain, S.: Nested linear/lattice codes for Wyner-Ziv encoding. In: Proceedings of Information Theory Workshop, Killarney, pp. 92–93 (1998)
27. Griod, B., Aaron, A., Rane, S.: Distributed video coding. Proc. IEEE 93(1), 71–83 (2005)
28. Aaron A., Zhang, R., Griod, B.: Wyner-Ziv coding of motion video. In: Proceedings of Asilomar Conference on Signals and Systems, Pacific Grove (2002)
29. Aaron, A., Rane, S., Griod, B.: Toward practical Wyner-ziv coding of video. In: Proceedings of IEEE International Conference on Image Proceeding, Barcelona, pp. 869–872 (2003)
30. Aaron A., Rane, S., Girod, B.: Wyner-Ziv coding for video: applications to compression and error resilience. In: Proceedings of IEEE Data Compression Conference, Snowbird, pp. 93–102 (2003)
31. Aaron, A., Rane, S., Setton, E., Griod, B.: Transform-domain Wyner-Ziv codec for video. In: Proceedings of Visual Communications and Image Processing, San Jose (2004)

32. Rebollo-Monedero, D., Aaron, A., Girod, B.: Transforms for high-rate distributed source coding. In: Proceedings of Asilomar Conference on Signals System and Computers, Pacific Grove (2003)
33. Puri, R., Ramchandran, K.: PRISM: a new robust video coding architecture based on distributed compression principles. In: Proceedings of Alleton Conference on Communication, Control, and Computing, Allerton (2002)
34. Puri, R., Ramchandran, K.: PRISM: an uplink-friendly multimedia coding paradigm. In: Proceedings of International Conference on Acoustics, Speech and Signal Processing, St Louis, pp. 856–859 (2003)
35. Puri, R., Ramchandran, K.: PRISM: a new reversed multimedia coding paradigm. In: Proceedings of IEEE International Conference on Image Processing, New York, pp. 617–620 (2003)
36. Fowler, J. E., Tagliasacchi, M., Pesquel-Popescu, B.: Wavelet-based distributed source coding of video. http://www.ee.bilkent.edu.tr/~signal/defevent/papers/cr1535.pdf. Accessed on October 29, 2001
37. Ascenso, J., Beites, C., Pereira, F.: Motion compensate refinement for low complexity pixel based on distributed video coding. http://www.img.lx.it.pt/~fp/artigos/AVSS_final.pdf. Accessed on October 29, 2001
38. Artigas, X., Ascenso, J., Dalai, M., et al.: The DISCOVER codec: architecture, techniques and evaluation. In: Proceedings of Picture Coding Symposium, Lisbon, pp. 1950–1953 (Nov 2007)
39. Pradhan, S.S., Kusuma, J., Ramchandran, K.: Distributed compression in a dense micro-sensor network. IEEE Signal Proc. Mag. **19**, 51–60 (2002)
40. Servetto, S. D., Lattice quantization with side information. In: Proceedings of IEEE Data Compression Conference, Snowbird, pp. 510–519 (Mar 2000)
41. Xiong, Z., Liveris, A., Cheng, S., Liu, Z.: Nested quantization and Slepian-Wolf coding: a Wyner-Ziv coding paradigm for i.i.d. sources. In: Proceedings of IEEE Workshop Statistical Signal Processing (SSP), St. Louis (2003)
42. Liu, Z., Cheng, S., Liveris, A. D., Xiong, Z.: Slepian-Wolf coded nested quantization (SWC-NQ) for Wyner-Ziv coding: performance analysis and code design. In: Proceedings of IEEE Data Compression Conference, Snowbird (Mar 2004)
43. Yang, Y., Cheng, S., Xiong Z., Zhao, W.: Wyner-Ziv coding based on TCQ and LDPC codes. In: Proceedings of Asilomar Conference on Signals, Systems and Computers, Pacific Grove (Nov 2003)
44. Flemming, M., Zhao, Q., Effros, M.: Network vector quantization. IEEE Trans. Inf. Theory **50**(8), 1584–1604 (2004)
45. Lloyd, S.P.: Least squares quantization in PCM. IEEE Trans. Inf. Theory **IT-28**, 129–1373 (1982)
46. Fleming, M., Effros, M.: Network vector quantization. In: Proceedings of IEEE Data Compression Conference, Snowbird, pp. 13–22 (2001)
47. Muresan, D., Effros, M.: Quantization as histogram segmentation: globally optimal scalar quantizer design in network system. In: Proceedings of IEEE Data Compression Conference, Snowbird, pp. 302–311 (2002)
48. Effros, M., Muresan, D.: Codecell contiguity in optimal fixed-rate and entropy-constrained network scalar quantizer. In: Proceedings of IEEE Data Compression Conference, Snowbird, pp. 312–321 (2002)
49. Cardinal, J., Asche, G. V.: Joint entropy-constrained multiterminal quantization. In: Proceedings of IEEE International Symposium on Information Theory (ISIT), Lausanne, p. 63 (2002)
50. Rebollo-Monedero, D., Aaron, A., Girod, B.: Transform for high-rate distributed source coding. In: Proceedings of Asilomar Conference Signals, System and Computers, Pacific Grove (2003)
51. Rebollo-Monedero, D., Zhang, R., Girod, B.: Design of optimal quantizers for distributed source coding. In: Proceedings of IEEE Data Compression Conference, Snowbird, pp. 13–22 (Mar 2003)

52. Tang, C., Cheung, N., Ortega, A., Raghavendra, C.: Efficient inter-band prediction and wavelet based compression for hyperspectral imagery: a distributed source coding approach. In: Proceedings of IEEE Data Compression Conference, Snowbird, pp. 437–446 (Mar 2005)

53. Pradhan, S. S., Ramchandran, K.: Distributed source coding using syndromes (DISCUS): design and construction. In: Proceedings of IEEE Data Compression Conference, Snowbird, pp. 158–167 (1999)

54. Pradhan, S., Ramchandran, K.: Distributed source coding: symmetric rates and applications to sensor networks. In: Proceedings of IEEE Data Compression Conference, Los Alamitos, pp. 363–372 (2000)

55. Pradhan, S. S., Ramchandran, K.: Group-theoretic construction and analysis of generalized coset codes for symmetric/asymmetric distributed source coding. In: Proceedings of Conference on Information Sciences and Systems, Princeton (Mar 2000)

56. Pradhan, S.S., Ramchandran, K.: Geometric proof of rate-distortion function of Gaussian source with side information at the decoder. In: Proceeding of IEEE International Symposium on Information Theory (ISIT), Piscataway, p. 351 (2000)

57. Wang, X., Orchard, M.: Design of trellis codes for source coding with side information at the decoder. In: Proceedings of IEEE Data Compression Conference, Snowbird, pp. 361–370 (2001)

58. Bajcsy, J., Mitran, P.: Coding for the Slepian–Wolf problem with turbo codes. In: Proceedings of IEEE Global Communications Conference, San Antonio (2001)

59. Aaron, A., Girod, B.: Compression with side information using turbo codes. In: Proceedings of IEEE Date Compression Conference, Snowbird, pp. 252–261 (Apr 2002)

60. Garcia-Frias, J., Zhao, Y.: Compression of correlated binary sources using turbo codes. IEEE Commun. Lett. **5**, 417–419 (2001)

61. Zhao, Y., Garcia-Frias, I.: Joint estimation and data compression of correlated nonbinary sources using punctured turbo codes. In: Proceedings of Information Science and System Conference, Princeton (2002)

62. Zhao, Y., Garcia-Frias, I.: Data compression of correlated nonbinary sources using punctured turbo codes. In: Proceedings of IEEE Data Compression Conference, Snowbird, pp. 242–251 (2002)

63. Mitran, P., Bajcsy, J.: Coding for the Wyner-Ziv problem with turbo-like codes. In: Proceedings of IEEE International Symposium on Information Theory, Lausanne, p. 91 (2002)

64. Mitran, P., Bajcsy, J.: Turbo source coding: a noise-robust approach to data compression. In: Proceedings of IEEE Data Compression Conference, Snowbird, p. 465 (2002)

65. Zhu, G., Alajaji, F.: Turbo codes for nonuniform memoryless sources over noisy channels. IEEE Commun. Lett. **6**(2), 64–66 (2002)

66. Schonberg, D., Pradhan, S.S., Ramchandran, K.: LDPC codes can approach the Slepian-Wolf bound for general binary sources. In: Proceedings of Allerton Conference Communication, Control, and Computing, Monticello (2002)

67. Leveris, A., Xiong, Z., Geolrghiades, C.: Compression of binary sources with side information at the decoder using LDPC codes. IEEE Commun. Lett. **6**(10), 440–442 (2002)

68. Varodayan, D., Aaron, A., Girod, B.: Rate-adaptive distributed source coding using low-density parity-check codes. In: Proceedings of Asilomar Conference on Signals, Systems and Computers, Pacific Grove, pp. 1–8 (2005)

69. Brites, C., Pereira, F.: Encoder rate control for transform domain Wyner-Ziv video coding. In: Proceedings of International Conference on Image Processing (ICIP), San Antonio, pp. 16–19 (Sept 2007)

70. Tonomura, Y., Nakachi, T., Fujii, T.: Efficient index assignment by improved bit probability estimation for parallel processing of distributed video coding. In: Proceedings of IEEE International Conference ICASSP, Las Vegas, pp. 701–704 (Mar 2008)

71. Bernardini, R., Rinaldo, R., Zontone, P., Alfonso, D., Vitali, A.: Wavelet domain distributed coding video. In: Proceedings of International Conference on Image Processing, Atlanta, pp. 245–248 (2006)

72. Bernardini, R., Rinaldo, R., Zontone, P., Vitali, A.: Performance evaluation of distributed video coding schemes. In: Proceedings of IEEE International Conference on Acoustics, Speech and Signal Processing, Las Vegas, pp. 709–712 (Mar 2008)
73. Morbee, M., Prades-Nebot, J., Pizurica, A., Philips, W.: Rate allocation algorithm for pixel-domain distributed video coding without feedback channel. In: Proceedings of IEEE ICASSP, Honolulu (Apr 2007)
74. Yaacoub, C., Farah, J., Pesquet-Popescu, B.: A cross-layer approach with adaptive rate allocation and quantization for return channel suppression in Wyner-Ziv video coding systems. In: Proceedings of 3rd International Conference on Information and Communication Technologies: From Theory to Applications (ICTTA), Damascus (2008)
75. Aaron, A., Rane, S., Girod, B.: Wyner-Ziv video coding with hash-based motion compensation at the receiver. In: Proceedings of IEEE International Conference on Image Processing, Singapore (2004)
76. Ascenso, J., Pereira, F.: Adaptive hash-based exploitation for efficiency Wyner-Ziv video coding. In: Proceedings of International Conference on Image Processing (ICIP), San Antonio, pp. 16–19 (Sept 2007)
77. Martinian, E., Vetro, A., Ascenso, J., Khisti, A., Malioutov, D.: Hybrid distributed video coding using SCA codes. In: Proceedings of IEEE 8th Workshop on Multimedia Signal Processing, Victoria, pp. 258–261 (2006)
78. Wang, A., Zhao, Y., Pan, J.S.: Residual distributed video coding based on LQR-Hash. Chinese J. Electron. **18**(1), 109–112 (2009)
79. Adikari, A. B. B., Fernando, W. A. C., Weerakkody, W. A. R. J., Kondoz, A. M.: SI joint spatial and temporal correlation exploitation for Wyner-Ziv frames coding in DVC. In: Proceedings of IEEE International Conference on Multimedia and Expo, Hannover, Germany, pp. 589–592 (Apr 2008)
80. Sun, Y., Tsai, C.: Low complexity motion model analysis for distributed video coding. In: Proceedings of International Wireless Communications and Mobile Computing Conference, IWCMC, Crete Island, pp. 437–440 (Aug 2008)
81. Dempster, A., Laird, N., Rubin, D.: Maximum likelihood from incomplete data via the EM algorithm. J. R. Stat. Soc. B **39**(1), 1–38 (1977)
82. Varodayan, D., Mavlankar, A., Flierl, M., Girod, B.: Distributed coding of random dot stereograms with unsupervised learning of disparity. In: Proceedings of IEEE International Workshop on Multimedia Signal Processing, Victoria (Oct 2006)
83. Varodayan, D., Lin, Y.-C., Mavlankar, A., Flierl, M., Girod, B.: Wyner-Ziv coding of stereo images with unsupervised learning of disparity. In: Proceedings of Picture Coding Symposium, Lisbon (Nov 2007)
84. Lin, C., Varodayan, D., Girod, B.: Spatial models for localization of image tampering using distributed source codes. In: Proceedings of Picture Coding Symposium, Lisbon (Nov 2007)
85. Lin, Y. C., Varodayan, D., Girod, B.: Image authentication and tampering localization using distributed source coding. In: Proceedings of IEEE International Workshop on Multimedia Signal Processing, MMSP 2007, Crete (Oct 2007)
86. Flierl, M., Girod, B.: Wyner-Ziv coding of video with unsupervised motion vector learning. Signal Proc. Image Commun. **23**(5), 369–378 (2008) (Special Issue Distributed Video Coding)
87. Chen, D., Varodayan, D., Flierl, M., Girod, B.: Wyner-Ziv coding of multiview images with unsupervised learning of disparity and Gray code. In: Proceedings of IEEE International Conference on Image Processing, San Diego (Oct 2008)
88. Bassi, F., Kieffer, M., Weidmann, C.: Source coding with intermittent and degraded side information at the decoder. In: Proceedings of ICASSP 2008, Las Vegas, pp. 2941–2944 (2008)
89. Brites, C., Pereira, F.: Correlation noise modeling for efficient pixel and transform domain Wyner-Ziv video coding. IEEE Trans. Circuits Syst. Video Technol. **18**(9), 1177–1190 (2008)
90. He, Z., Cao, L., Cheng, H.: Correlation estimation and performance optimization for distributed image compression. In: Proceedings of SPIE Visual Communications and Image Processing, San Jose (2006)

91. Hua, G., Chen, C. W.: Distributed video coding with zero motion skip and efficient DCT coefficient encoding. In: Proceedings of IEEE International Conference on Multimedia and Expo, Hannover, pp. 777–780 (Apr 2008)
92. Weerakkody, W. A. R. J., Fernando, W. A. C., Kondoz, A. M.: An enhanced reconstruction algorithm for unidirectional distributed video coding. In: Proceedings of IEEE International Symposium on Consumer Electronics, Algarve, pp. 1–4 (Apr 2008)

Chapter 2
Principles of MDC

2.1 Introduction

To design the MDC, the difficult point is that different from the traditional single-description coding, the latter only needs to consider the rate distortion function of two variables $R(D)$, but the former (in the circumstance of two descriptions) should take comprehensive consideration of the five elements' function $(R_1, R_2, D_0, D_1, D_2)$. On the one hand, if according to the traditional single-description method to optimize the design of the two single-channel transmission rate R_1, R_2 and single-channel distortion D_1, D_2, then the synthesis of the two descriptions of the two-way transmission rate $R_1 + R_2$ and dual distortion D_0 can hardly be an optimized encoding scheme. On one hand, if according to the traditional single-description method to make the transmission rate $R_1 + R_2$ and dual distortion D_0 to achieve optimum design, then the descriptions divided by the bit stream $R_1 + R_2$ are hard to achieve optimum design. The realization scope of the five elements' function $(R_1, R_2, D_0, D_1, D_2)$ has the following restraints:

$$D_0 \geq D(R_1 + R_2) \tag{2.1}$$

$$D_1 \geq D(R_1) \tag{2.2}$$

$$D_2 \geq D(R_2) \tag{2.3}$$

Among the above, (2.1), (2.2), and (2.3) can never take equal signs at the same time; in the next section, we will show the rate-distortion zone of MDC $(R_1, R_2, D_0, D_1, D_2)$ from the perspective of information theory.

H. Bai et al., *Distributed Multiple Description Coding*,
DOI 10.1007/978-1-4471-2248-7_2, © Springer-Verlag London Limited 2011

2.2   Relative Information Theory

2.2.1   The Traditional Rate-Distortion Function

As for the distortion coding, rate distortion gives the reachable minimum code rate $R(D)$ under the circumstance that the qualified distortion is less than D [1–3].

Assume that the signal source x consists of a series of independent real random variables with same distribution $x_1, x_2, \ldots, x_n$; the reconstruction of distortion is d, given a nonnegative number $d(x, \widehat{x})$; measure the similarity between a signal source x and the reconstruction $\widehat{x}$. Then the distortion of $x^{(n)} = (x_1, x_2, \ldots, x_n)$ and $\widehat{x}^{(n)} = (\widehat{x}_1, \widehat{x}_2, \ldots, \widehat{x}_n)$ can be defined as:

$$d\left(x^{(n)}, \widehat{x}^{(n)}\right) = \frac{1}{n} \sum_{i=1}^{n} d(x_i, \widehat{x}_i). \tag{2.4}$$

Among them, n is the length of sequence. The most common distortion is squared error-based distortion:

$$d(x, \widehat{x}) = (x - \widehat{x})^2 \tag{2.5}$$

As for a sequence n in length, $x^{(n)}$, the encoder α maps the signal source sequence with the speed R to a group of index $\{1, 2, \ldots, 2^{nR}\}$; then use the decoder β to map the index $\{1, 2, \ldots, 2^{nR}\}$ to the reconstruction sequence $\widehat{x}^{(n)}$; the occurrence of distortion is the combined effects of signal source and reconstruction:

$$D = E[d(x^n, \widehat{x}^{(n)})] = E[d(x^n, \beta(\alpha(x^n)))]. \tag{2.6}$$

In the case of qualified distortion D, the rate distortion $R(D)$ is the reachable minimum code rate; on the contrary, in the case of the qualified transmission code rate R, the rate-distortion function is the reachable maximum distortion [1–3].

For signal sources with any probability distribution, it is difficult to find out the explicit formulation of $R(D)$ or $D(R)$, but for the relatively simple and representative non-memory Gaussian sources, set the variance as σ^2, measure the distortion-rate function with squared error-based distortion, and the result is:

$$D(R) = \sigma^2 2^{-2R}. \tag{2.7}$$

For the distribution density function $f(x)$ and the signal source with σ^2 as its variance, measure it with squared error-based; the distortion-rate function is:

$$\frac{1}{2\pi e} 2^{2h} 2^{-2R} \leq D(R) \leq \sigma^2 2^{-2R} \tag{2.8}$$

Among them, $h = -\int f(x) \log_2 f(x) dx$ is called entropy, the upper limit of (2.8) shows that for a given variance, the Gaussian sources are most difficult to compress.

2.2.2 The Rate-Distortion Function of MDC

The multiple-description rate distortion region is a closed interval for certain sources and distortion measurement. In the case of two descriptions, multiple-description region is a closed interval expressed by $(R_1, R_2, D_0, D_1, D_2)$.

The theory of Gamal and Cover [4] answers how to get a reachable five-element interval from the simultaneous distribution of signal source and random variance of reconstruction. Ozarow [5] proved that the multiple-description region is the optimal set which meets the theory of Gamal and Cover; any multiple-description region of consistent non-memory sources measured by squared error can be restricted by the multiple-description region of Gaussian signal sources.

For the non-memory Gaussian sources with the variance of σ^2, the multiple-description region $(R_1, R_2, D_0, D_1, D_2)$ meet the following terms [6, 7]:

$$D_i \geq \sigma^2 2^{-2R_i}, \ i = 1, 2 \tag{2.9}$$

$$D_0 \geq \sigma^2 2^{-2(R_1 + R_2)} \gamma_D (R_1, R_2, D_1, D_2) \tag{2.10}$$

Among them, when $D_1 + D_2 > \sigma^2 + D_0$, $\gamma_D = 1$, or else

$$\gamma_D = \frac{1}{1 - \left(\sqrt{(1 - D_1)(1 - D_2)} - \sqrt{D_1 D_2 - 2^{-2(R_1 + R_2)}}\right)^2} \tag{2.11}$$

Formula 2.10 indicates that the center distortion will not be less than γ_D times the minimum distortion rate. When one or two single channels are larger, $\gamma_D = 1$, reconstruction of the center can get very good results. Here, something must be classified – the right of Formulas 2.9 and 2.10 gives the minimum distortion in theory; the actual system is usually beyond the bottom line.

In the two channels balanced situation, that is, $R_1 = R_2$ and $D_1 = D_2$, meet:

$$D_1 \geq \min \left\{ \frac{1}{2} \left[1 + D_0 - (1 - D_0) \sqrt{1 - 2^{-2(R_1 + R_2)} / D_0} \right], \right.$$
$$\left. 1 - \sqrt{1 - 2^{-2(R_1 + R_2)} / D_0} \right\} \tag{2.12}$$

At this time, also meet $D_1 > \sigma^2 2^{-2R_1}$.

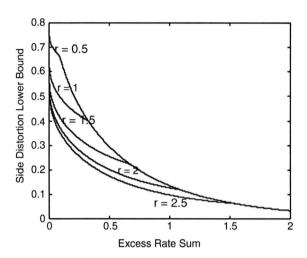

Fig. 2.1 Redundancy vs. side distortion lower bound at different base rate [31]

If the redundancy is expressed as

$$\rho = R_1 + R_2 - R(D_0), \qquad (2.13)$$

then it can be said by basic code rate $r = R(D_0)$ and redundancy ρ:

$$D_1 \geq \begin{cases} \dfrac{1}{2}[1 + 2^{-2r} - (1 - 2^{-2r})\sqrt{1 - 2^{-2\rho}}], & for\ \rho \leq r - 1 + \log_2(1 + 2^{-2r}) \\ \sqrt{1 - 2^{-2\rho}}, & for\ \rho > r - 1 + \log_2(1 + 2^{-2r}). \end{cases}$$
$$(2.14)$$

Equation 2.14 can be described by Fig. 2.1 specifically, that is, the relationship between the redundancy and single-channel distortion in different basic code rate. As evident, when the basic code rate is under certain circumstances, the greater the amount of redundancy, the smaller is the single-channel distortion. When the amount of redundancy is low, the slope of D_1 is

$$\frac{\partial D_1}{\partial \rho} = -\frac{1 - 2^{-2r}}{2} \frac{2^{-2\rho} \ln 2}{\sqrt{1 - 2^{-2\rho}}}. \qquad (2.15)$$

Among the parameters, when $\rho = 0^+$, the slope is inexhaustible. This infinite slope value means that a little increase in the code bit can make the single-channel distortion fall more sharply than the center distortion. This also indicates that the multiple-description system should be nonzero redundancy.

The redundancy of MDC is represented by Formula 2.13. If the redundant information ρ is zero, then it returns to the general single-description coding; its disadvantage is it demands signal channel of high quality and cannot carry out error recovery to an unreliable channel. If ρ reaches the highest value, then it equals the code rate of a single description, equivalent to transmit the single description through the different channel twice. There is no independent information among the various descriptions, it fails to achieve complementary enhanced, center decoding equivalent to the single-channel decoding effect of using only one description. Therefore, to coordinate the independence and correlation among descriptions is the key to MDC.

2.3 Review of MDC

2.3.1 Subsampling-Based MDC

The MDC based on subsampling [8–19] divides the original signal into several subsets on space domain, time domain, or frequency domain; each subset is transmitted as different descriptions. The MDC method based on subsampling mainly takes advantage of the smoothing characteristic of image or video signals, that is, apart from the border area. The adjacent pixel values in space or time are related or change smoothly. Therefore, a description can be estimated by others.

In the early research of Bell Labs [20], they used the method of parity sampling for video source to realize the separation of signal channels, generating two descriptions, as shown in Fig. 2.2.

Representative algorithms include: frame sampling in time domain [9, 10], the space-pixel-mixed algorithm applied to image sampling points [11, 17] or motion vector [14] and mixed algorithm of transform coefficients [12, 13, 19].

In the simplest time domain subsampling method [9], according to the odd–even frame, the input video sequence was sampled to two subsequences to transmit, and each subsequence can decode independently. Wenger [10] proposed the algorithm of VRC, and was supported by H.263+ and recommended by ITU-T.

Franchi et al. [17] designed two structures of multiple-description coding – these two structures are all prediction loop based on motion compensation – and used polyphase down-sampling technique to produce a description of each other

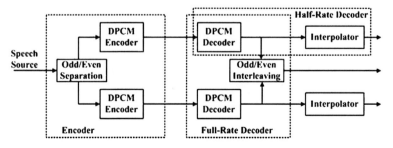

Fig. 2.2 Speech coding for channel splitting as proposed by Jayant [20]

redundant; they adopted a prefilter to control redundancy and single-channel distortion. The first proposal is DC-MDVC (Drift-Compensation Multiple Description Video Coder); it can realize robustness in an unreliable network, but it can only provide two descriptions. The second proposal is IF-MDVC (Independent Flow Multiple Description Video Coder). Before, the motion compensation circulating it produced multiple data collections; in this case, the amount of descriptions used by the encoder has no strict restrictions. If we do not use the prefilter, the redundancy and single-channel distortion of sampling algorithm for multiple description are controlled by the statistical characteristic of the signal source.

Based on the research on video compression standards, Kim and Lee [14] used the motion-compensated prediction technology to remove the higher time correlation of a real image sequence. Motion vector field is one of the most important data in the compressed bit stream; its loss will seriously affect the quality of decoding reconstruction. The proposed multiple-description motion coding in this paper can enhance the robustness of the motion vector field when transmission error occurs. In MDMC, the motion vector field was separated into two descriptions, which transmit on two signal channels. In the decoder end, even if there is a description loss in the process of transmission, it is able to restore an acceptable predicting image; if both descriptions are received accurately, then the decoder is able to restore an image with higher quality.

Bajic and Woods [18] considered the strategy of optimized segmentation that separates every signal area into subsets and sets the distance from the center of one subset to another as far as possible. In cases of certain package-loss rate, this distributed packaging mechanism is able to use simple error concealment algorithm to produce acceptable effect even without the use of FEC or other forms of additional redundancy. Experimental results show that the distribution packaging mechanism is suitable for image and video transmission on unreliable network.

2.3.2 Quantization-Based MDC

The multiple-description coding algorithms based on quantization mainly include the multiple-description scalar quantization [21] and the multiple-description lattice vector quantization [22].

Vaishampayan [21] developed the theory of MDSQ and applied it to the problem of combat channel transmission error in communication system. In MDSQ, Vaishampayan combined the scalar quantization with encoding and divided the multiple-description coding into two steps: the first step is scalar quantization and the second step is index allocation, represented as $\alpha_0 = \ell \circ \alpha$, where scalar quantization process α can be realized by an ordinary scalar quantizer with a fixed rate; index allocation process ℓ assigned a group of quantitative indexes (i_1, i_2) for each scalar sampling x, which is a map from one-dimensional to two-dimensional $I : N \to N \times N$. The map can be represented by a matrix called index allocation matrix, as shown in Fig. 2.3. The quantitative coefficients correspond to the point

Fig. 2.3 Index assignment for MDSQ

a

	000	001	010	011	100	101	110	111
000	0							
001	1	2						
010		3	4					
011			5	6				
100				7	8			
101					9	10		
110						11	12	
111							13	14

b

	000	001	010	0111	100	101
000	0	1				
001	2	3	5			
010		4	6	7		
011			8	9	11	
100				10	12	13
101					14	15

c

	00	01	10	11
00	0	1	5	6
01	2	4	7	12
10	3	8	11	13
11	9	10	14	15

of the matrix row and column labels which make up the index of the coefficients (i_1, i_2). The index allocation ℓ must be reversible to reconstruct the signal and it can be represented by ℓ^{-1}. In the decoder end, three decoders β_0, β_1, and β_2 start the signal reconstruction from $(i_1, i_2), i_1$, and i_2, respectively. As for the situation of two descriptions, when the receiving end receives two descriptions at the same time, we can use the center decoder β_0, according to the index (i_1, i_2) and restore the factor values accurately. When the receiving end only receives one description, you can seek out the approximate value according to index of rows or columns by using the single-channel decoder β_1 or β_2. The index allocation is subject to the following rules: the x elements are encoded from 0 to $x - 1$ after being quantified by α, and they begin to fill from upper left to lower right, from the main diagonal to the outside. The scope of quantitative coefficients distribution is represented by the number of occupied diagonals.

The simplest quantization matrix is $A(2)$, the number of diagonals is 2, as shown in Fig. 2.3. The quantitative values encoded are from 0 to 14 and are assigned to 8×8 index matrix. If it is central channel decoding, we can get accurate reconstruction by using the index (i_1, i_2); if it is single-channel decoding, we can only reconstruct it by using row index i_1 or column index i_2 and it may produce single-channel distortion with a value of 1 (e.g., according to the row index 101 to reconstruct, the possible coefficients are 9,10 with the difference of 1). Because the index matrix with 64 units only contains 15 quantitative coefficients, the redundancy is considerable. Figure 2.3b is the index matrix of $A(3)$, the number of diagonal is 3, and the 16 quantitative coefficients are assigned to index matrix of 6×6; it is index allocation relative to low redundancy. If conducting single-channel decoding, the maximum distortion is 3 (e.g., reconstruct according to column index 100 and the possible coefficients are 11, 12, 14, the maximum difference is 3). The index allocation matrix of Fig. 2.3c is full, which indicates that if there is no redundancy, then the distortion is large, up to 9. The key to the scheme of multiple-description scalar quantization is how to design an index allocation matrix.

The method mentioned above is the method of using scalar quantization to form MDC. Formally, the multiple-description scalar quantization can be applied to vector quantization without amendment, for the vector with N in length, the relative scope of α (the scope of encoder) and the decoder $\beta_0 \ \beta_1 \ \beta_2$ is R^N. However, with the increase of dimension N, the encoding complexity will exponentially increase. In addition, due to the disorder of the coding vector, the index allocation ℓ in MDSQ cannot be directly extended to MDVQ, making the problem of index allocation very complex.

Therefore, Servetto et al. proposed the multiple-description lattice vector quantization [22]. They applied the lattice structure and gave a proposal to solve the issue of multiple-description vector quantization: select grid point $\Lambda \subset R^N$, subgrid point $\Lambda' \subset \Lambda$. The subgrid point is to determine the reconstruction value of the single-channel decoder and is obtained by rotating and scaling the grid point. At this time, quantizer α turns into a lattice vector quantization process from the complex vector quantization, and the optimal index allocation $\ell : \Lambda \rightarrow \Lambda' \times \Lambda'$ can be defined in the center of a cell, and then be extended to the entire space through the translation symmetry of lattice. In short, in the method of MDLVQ, lattice geometry structure not only simplifies the problem of index allocation but also reduces code complexity. The specific MDLVQ plan is highlighted in Chap. 4.

2.3.3 Transform-Based MDC

The transform-based MDC is a multiple-description coding scheme [23] proposed by Wang et al. from the perspective of sub-space mapping. The proposal contains two transformation processes: the signal source through the decorrelation trans-forms (such as DCT and so on), then conducts linear transformation on the transform coefficients. The latter is called relative transformation, represented by T. In this way, the transform coefficients are divided into a number of groups; coefficients between different groups are related. A simple example of relative transformation is:

$$\begin{bmatrix} y_1 \\ y_2 \end{bmatrix} = \begin{bmatrix} \theta & (2\theta)^{-1} \\ -\theta & (2\theta)^{-1} \end{bmatrix} \begin{bmatrix} x_1 \\ x_2 \end{bmatrix}. \tag{2.16}$$

Among them, x_1 and x_2 are independent Gaussian random variables, θ is a positive real number, and the variance distribution are σ_1^2 and σ_2^2 and $\sigma_1^2 > \sigma_2^2$. The relative transformation transforms the noncorrelation vector x into correlation vector y. You can prove that the following relation is true:

$$E(y_1 y_2) = -\theta^2 \sigma_1^2 + (2\theta)^{-2} \sigma_2^2. \tag{2.17}$$

Here, $E(y_1 y_2)$ means calculate cross-correlation of y_1 and y_2 only when

$$\theta^4 = (4\sigma_1^2)^{-1} \sigma_2^2 \tag{2.18}$$

or else, $E(y_1 y_2) \neq 0$. This indicates that y_1 and y_2 are interrelated, and uses the correlation of the transform coefficients to construct multiple-description coding. When some descriptions are lost, you can still use the correlation to estimate them, such as using the linear Bayesian estimation and so on. Making use of the performance of relative transformation, we design the MDC based on relative transformation.

In order to simplify the design of transformation, Wang applied the pair-wise correlation to transform to each pair of nonrelated coefficients. The two coefficients of PCT were separated into two descriptions, then coded independently. If you receive two descriptions, then seek the reverse PCT transformation of each two transform coefficients; in this case you can restore the original volume which exists by quantization error only. If we receive only one description, coefficients of the lost descriptions can be estimated according to the correlation of the coefficients. The optimal relative transformation under the fixed redundancy to make the least distortion of single description has the following form:

$$T = \begin{bmatrix} \sqrt{\dfrac{\cot\theta}{2}} & \sqrt{\dfrac{\tan\theta}{2}} \\ -\sqrt{\dfrac{\cot\theta}{2}} & \sqrt{\dfrac{\tan\theta}{2}} \end{bmatrix}. \tag{2.19}$$

Among them, parameter θ is determined by the size of redundancy introduced by each two variables. When adding a small amount of redundancy and transformation, very good results are achievable and by adding a large number of redundancy the results are not that good. If you want to encode $N \geq 2$ variables, there exists an optimal matching strategy. It is necessary to measure by multiple-description redundancy rate-distortion function and cooperate with the optimal redundancy among the selected couplet, for the given total redundancy to make the sum of distortion of single description to the minimum.

2.3.4 FEC-Based MDC

The basic idea of the FEC-based MDC is to divide the signal source code stream into data segments of different importance, then use different numbers of FEC channel code data to protect different data segments and through a certain mechanism of packaging to turn the signal channel code stream with priorities into nonpriority data segments. For example, for scalable coding, Puri and Ramchandran [24] proposed the use of the gradually weakened FEC channel encoding for the declining importance levels, and turning of a bit stream of gradual change into a robust multiple-description bit stream. Mohr and Riskin [25] used FEC of different levels to prevent data loss, and according to the importance of information in scalable encoding to the image quality, they allocated appropriate redundancy for every description. The FEC-based unequal error protection algorithm in [24] and [25] mainly targets the scalable source encoding. Varnic and Fleming [26] used the cycle description of the state information in the encoder part rather than the traditional method of error protection to protect SPIHT coding bit stream, using the iteration algorithm in decoding end to rectify the destroyed bit stream.

Sachs Raghavan and Ramchandran [27] adopted the cascade channel coding to construct an MDC method which can be applied to a network where packet loss and bit error exist; the external coding is based on RCPC encoding with cyclic redundancy check while the internal coding of source channel consists of a SPIHT encoder and an FEC coding of optimal unequal error protection. Bajic and Woods [28] combined the domain-based MDC and FEC-based MDC and arrived at a better system. Zhang and Motani [29] combined the DCT which distinguish priorities and the FEC-based multiple description; in addition, Miguell and Mohr [30] applied the compression algorithm of image into a multiple-description framework, added the controlled redundancy into the original data during the process of compression to overcome data loss and adjust redundancy in accordance with the importance of data to realize unequal error protection.

2.4 Summary

First, this chapter described the basic idea of MDC from the perspective of information theory. We introduced the basic theory of MDC and its difference from traditional single-description coding, and also outlined the existing MDC method, which includes: MDC based on subsampling, MDC based on quantization, MDC based on relative transformation, and MDC based on FEC.

References

1. Berger, T.: Rate Distortion Theory. Prentice-Hall, Englewood Cliffs (1971)
2. Cover, T.M., Thomas, J.A.: Elements of Information Theory. Wiley, New York (1991)
3. Gray, R.M.: Source Coding Theory. Kluwer, Boston (1990)
4. El Gamal, A.A., Cover, T.M.: Achievable rates for multiple descriptions. IEEE Trans. Inf. Theory **28**, 851–857 (1982)
5. Ozarow, L.: On a source-coding problem with two channels and three receivers. Bell Syst. Tech. J. **59**(10), 1909–1921 (1980)
6. Zamir, R.: Gaussian codes and Shannon bounds for multiple descriptions. IEEE Trans. Inf. Theory **45**, 2629–2635 (1999)
7. Linder, T., Zamir, R., Zeger, K.: The multiple description rate region for high resolution source coding. In: Proceedings of IEEE Data Compression Conference, Snowbird, pp. 149–158 (Mar– Apr 1998)
8. Ingle, A., Vaishanmpayan, V.A.: DPCM system design for diversity systems with application to packetized speech. IEEE Trans. Speech Audio Proc. **3**, 48–58 (1995)
9. Apostolopoulos, J.G.: Error-resillient video compression through the use of multiple states. In: Proceedings of IEEE International Conference on Image Processing, Vancouver, vol. 3, pp. 352–355 (Sept 2000)
10. Wenger, S.: Video redundancy coding in H.263+. Presented at the Audio-Visual Services Over Packet Networks Conference, Aberdeen (1997)
11. Wang, Y., Chung, D.: Non-hierarchical signal decomposition and maximally smooth reconstruction for wireless video transmisstion. In: Goodman, D., Raychaudhri, D. (eds.) Mobile Mutimedia Communications, pp. 285–292. Plenum, New York (1997)
12. Chung, D., Wang, Y.: Mutiple description image coding using signal decompostion and reconstruction based on lapped orthogonal transforms. IEEE Trans. Circuits Syst. Video Technol. **9**, 895–908 (1999)
13. Chung, D., Wang, Y.: Lapped orthogonal transforms designed for error resilient image coding. IEEE Trans. Circuits Syst. Video Technol. **12**, 752–764 (2002)
14. Kim, C., Lee, S.: Multiple description coding of motion fields for robust video transmission. IEEE Trans. Circuits Syst. Video Technol. **11**, 999–1010 (2001)
15. Apostolopoulos, J.: Reliable video communication over lossy packet networks using multiple state encoding and path diversity. In: Proceedings of Visual Communications and Image Processing, San Jose, pp. 392–409 (2001)
16. Wang, Y., Lin, S.: Error resilient video coding using multiple description motion compensation. IEEE Trans. Circuits Syst. Video Technol. **12**, 438–453 (2002)
17. Franchi, N., et al.: Multiple description coding for scalar and robust transmission over IP. Presented at the Packet Video Conference, Nantes (2003)
18. Bajic, I.V., Woods, J.W.: Domain-based multiple description coding to images and video. IEEE Trans. Image Proc. **12**, 1211–1225 (2003)
19. Cho, S., Pearlman, W.A.: A full-featured, error resilient, scalar wavelet video codec based on the set partitioning in hierarchical trees (SPIHT) algorithm. IEEE Trans. Circuits Syst. Video Technol. **12**, 157–170 (2002)
20. Jayant, N.S.: Subsampling of a DPCM speech channel to provide two'self-contained' half-rate channels. Bell Syst. Tech. J. **60**(4), 501–509 (1981)
21. Vaishanmpayan, V.A.: Design of multiple description scalar quantizers. IEEE Trans. Inf. Theory **39**(3), 821–834 (1993)

22. Servetto, S.D., Vaishampayan, V.A., Sloan, N.J.A.: Multiple description lattice vector quanti-
    zation. In: IEEE Data Compression Conference, Snowbird, pp. 13–22 (Mar 1999)
23. Wang, Y., Orchard, M.T., Vaishampayan, V., Reibman, A.R.: Multiple description coding using
    pairwise correlating transform. IEEE Trans. Image Proc. **10**(3), 351–366 (2001)
24. Puri, R., Ramchandran, K.: Multiple description source coding using forward error correction
    codes. In: Conference Record of the Thirty-third Asilomar Conference on Signals Systems and
    Computers, Pacific Grove, pp. 342–346 (1999)
25. Mohr, A.E., Riskin, E.A., Landerm, R.E.: Generalized multiple description through unequal
    loss protection. In: Proceedings of International Conference on Image Processing, Kobe,
    pp. 411–415 (1999)
26. Varnica, N., Fleming, M., Effros, M.: Multi-resolution adaptation of the spiht algorithm for
    multiple description. In: Proceedings of Data Compression Conference, Snowbird, pp. 303–
    312 (2000)
27. Sachs, D.G., Anand, R., Ramchandran, K.: Wireless image transmission using multiple
    description based concatenated codes. In: Proceedings of Data Compression Conference,
    Snowbird, p. 569 (2000)
28. Bajic, V., Woods, J.W.: Concatenated multiple description coding of frame rate scalable video.
    In: Proceedings of International Conference on Image Processing, New York, pp. 193–196
    (2002)
29. Zhang, Y., Motani, M., Garg, H.K.: Wireless video transmission using multiple description
    codes combined with prioritized DCT compression. In: Proceedings of IEEE International
    Conference on Multimedia and Expo, Lausanne, pp. 261–264 (2002)
30. Miguell, A.C., Mohr, A.E., Riskin, E.A.: Spiht for generalized multiple description coding. In:
    Proceedings of International Conference on Image Processing, Kobe, pp. 842–846 (1999)
31. Goyal, V.K.: Multiple description coding: compression meets the network. IEEE Signal Proc.
    Mag. **18**(5), 74–93 (2001)

Chapter 3
Principles of DVC

3.1 Relative Information Theory

DVC is the important application of DSC for video coding. This chapter introduces
the relative information theory of DSC. Then, on the basis of these corresponding
theories, one of the most significant principles of DSC, that is, Slepian–Wolf coding
is presented based on Turbo and LDPC, respectively. Finally, the performance of
Slepian–Wolf coding is analyzed in detail.

In order to make a comparative analysis of the principles of DSC, this section
analyzes several cases of two correlative source coding, as shown in Fig. 3.1,
assuming that X and Y are two statistically dependent i.i.d. finite-alphabet random
sequences.

3.1.1 Independent Coding, Independent Decoding

As shown in Fig. 3.1, with separate conventional entropy encoders and decoders,
X and Y may be encoded using lossless coding at the bit rate of $R_X \geq H(X)$ and
$R_Y \geq H(Y)$, respectively, and their total bit rate is $R_X + R_Y \geq H(X) + H(Y)$.
Here, $H(X)$ and $H(Y)$ are the entropies of sequence X and Y, respectively.

3.1.2 Joint Coding, Joint Decoding

As shown in Fig. 3.1, according to the information theory, X and Y can be encoded
using joint lossless coding at the bit rate of conditional entropy $R_X \geq H(X|Y)$
and $R_Y \geq H(Y|X)$, respectively, and the total bit rate is their joint entropy $R_X +
R_Y \geq H(X,Y)$.

H. Bai et al., *Distributed Multiple Description Coding*,
DOI 10.1007/978-1-4471-2248-7_3, © Springer-Verlag London Limited 2011

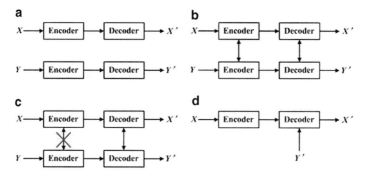

Fig. 3.1 Some cases of two dependent sources, (**a**) separated encoding and decoding, (**b**) joint encoding and decoding, (**c**) separated encoding and joint decoding, (**d**) WZ coding with side information accessible at decoder only

Fig. 3.2 Rate range of X and Y in distributed source coding [1]

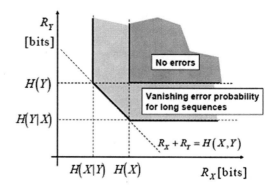

3.1.3 Independent Coding, Joint Decoding

In DSC, as shown in Fig. 3.1, according to theory of Slepian–Wolf [1] at this time, the accessible rate is shown in Fig. 3.2. If it can tolerate a certain amount of error when restoring X and Y, and the probability of error can be arbitrarily small when the coding sequence is long enough (generally considered to be zero), then we can also do independent encoding without distortion by using code rate $R_X \geq H(X|Y)$ and $R_Y \geq H(Y|X)$ separately in theory, in which case the total bit rate can reach joint entropy $R_X + R_Y \geq H(X,Y)$. That is to say, although we conduct independent coding for X and Y, the total bit rate can still reach the joint entropy $H(X,Y)$, the code rate adopts joint coding and decoding for X and Y, and this is the theoretical basis of lossless DSC. Furthermore, Wyner and Ziv [2] extended this theory to situations where distortion exists: as for the related Gaussian sources X and Y, if the distortion is calculated by mean square error, then the rate distortion function of independent coding joint decoding is same as that of joint coding and decoding; but for the source of general statistical distribution and the mean square error of measurement, the Zamir's theory [3] proved that the difference between WZ bit rate and the rate of joint coding joint decoding is not >0.5 bits/sample point; on binary source and Hamming distance, the difference is <0.22 bits/sample point.

3.1.4 Side Information Encoding in the Decoder

In Fig. 3.1, as the special case of form 3, assuming that the source Y has been restored without distortion, the coding end considers the rate distortion function of X only. Corresponding to the inflection point in Fig. 3.2, its corresponding lossless bit rate is $R_X \geq H(X|Y), R_Y = H(Y)$.

3.2 Distributed Source Coding

According to the above comparison, DSC can be defined as an issue of independent joint coding and decoding for two (or more) related sources; specifically speaking, the coding end uses an independent encoder for each signal source, and each encoder sends the coded bit stream to the decoder separately; the decoder does joint decoding by taking advantage of statistical correlation of various signal sources. This structure of DSC provided the theory guarantee for simplifying the coding end; thus, we can shift the complex operations of de-correlation to the decoding end.

The implementation of DSC includes two cases: one is lossless encoding which is based on the theory of Slepian–Wolf and is called Slepian–Wolf coding; the second is the realization when having distortion, which is based on the theory of WZ and so is called WZ encoding. In general, WZ encoder consists of a quantizer and a Slepian–Wolf encoder. The following examples show the implementation and feasibility of Slepian–Wolf coding. Suppose there are two 3-bit sources which are correlated, equal probability distribution and the correlation between them shows that the code distance $d_H(X, Y) \leq 1$. If Y is known at both ends of coding and decoding, you can encode X as 2 bits (because the mold 2 plus of X and Y has four kinds of possible cases – (000),(001),(010),(100), 2 bits is enough). While in the case of the coding end cannot get Y and only the decoding end can get Y, you can still compress X into 2 bits. The basis is if you already know $X = (000)$ or $X = (111)$, then there is no need to spend a bit to distinguish these two values because only one of them satisfy $d_H(X,Y) \leq 1$. In fact, you can put $X = (000)$ and $X = (111)$ into a coset. Similarly, dividing the other codeword in the space of 3-bit binary codeword into three additional different cosets is making the hamming distance between the two codewords in every company set greater than or equal to 2. Because there are four cosets in all, only 2 bits are needed to be specified, then which coset X belongs to; these four cosets are:

- coset $1 = (000, 111)$ the mapping is 00.
- coset $2 = (001, 110)$ the mapping is 01.

- coset $3 = (010, 101)$ the mapping is 10.
- coset $4 = (011, 100)$ the mapping is 11.

The decoder end reverts to the codeword nearest to the hamming distance of Y in the coset. The above examples illustrate that the coding end can also be compressed to 2 bit even without the information of Y. For example, when $X = 001, Y = 011$ (when it meets the condition $d_H(X,Y) \leq 1$), mapping it to coset 2, it is encoded as 01 and is sent to the decoder end, according to the received $Y = 011$ and $d_H(X,Y) \leq 1$ in the decoding end, then we can figure out that it can only be $X = 001$ and can never be $X = 110$ in coset 2.

The above example simply demonstrates the feasibility of Slepian–Wolf encoding; although Slepian–Wolf coding is a source coding issue, the problem, in fact, is closely related to channel coding. The key issue of Slepian–Wolf encoder is the segmentation of the source codeword space. Divide the output of source X into different groups which are called cosets; this kind of division makes the minimum distance between two codewords to the maximum as possible and, at the same time, maintains the symmetry of the coset. The encoder through the transmission of coset index to achieve the purpose of the data compression, the codec searches and gets the codeword closest to the side information as the decoding results, but this kind of division can be interpreted by the concept of channel codes.

Consider two binary sequences X and Y, assuming the sequence $u = X \oplus Y$, if sequence X is very similar to Y, then most data of the sequence u are 0, and only a small part are 1 to represent the position of X, Y from when the values are different. First of all, explain DSC from the perspective of channel code syndrome: regard X as a codeword of linear block channel codes, multiply X by the check matrix of channel code and generate the syndrome; send the syndrome to the decoding end, the receiving end search the sequence nearest to the side information Y as the recovery value of X in the coset expressed by the syndrome. Here, we realize the division of the above codeword by using the channel codeword syndrome. Because the number of bits of the syndrome is less than the number of bits of X, it is, thus, available for compression. Then, from the perspective of channel error-correcting code check bits (parity) [4], in order to "protect" sequence X and conduct channel coding, such as the systematic turbo coding, it generates information bits and parity bits, but we only transmit the parity bits. In the decoding end, take advantage of the statistical characteristics of sequences X and Y, conduct error-correcting decoding by using the combination of the receiving parity bits and side information Y, if sequences X and Y have higher similarities.

We only need to transmit a few parity bits to restore X so that we can get higher compression. But something must be emphasized – this is not used as the forward error correction (FEC) to protect the error occurred during "effective channel" transmission but a source coding method to recover the primary information X by side information Y, assuming that there is a "virtual related noise channel" between X and Y. This method realizes the segmentation of the above codeword by the channel parity bits. In fact, these two explanations are consistent, for example, use the parity bit to explain, the Coder sends a binary row vector $P_a = XP$, in which $G = [I|P]$ is a generated matrix of a systematic linear block codes, use the conception of syndrome to explain, the encoder sends the syndrome $S,S = XH$, in which H is the parity matrix of linear block codes; if $P = H$, then the transmitted binary stream will be the same.

Next, we will describe the implementation of two Slepian–Wolf encoders with high performance.

3.3 Turbo-Based Slepian–Wolf Coding

3.3.1 Problem Description

Now, consider the compression problem of joint coding of two independent identical distribution binary related sources X and Y, in which $X = (x_1,x_2,\ldots,x_K)$, $Y = (y_1,y_2,\ldots,y_K)$, and $x_i,y_i \in \{0,1\}$.

$$p(x_i = 0) = p(x_i = 1) = 1/2$$

$$p(y_i = 0) = p(y_i = 1) = 1/2$$

Setting that x_i is only related to $y_i (i \in [1,2,\ldots K])$ and is not related to $y_j (j \neq i)$, while the correlation between sources X and Y is fully described by conditional probability $P(X|Y)$, and assuming that source Y has been compressed by the traditional methods of entropy coding and has been restored without distortion, the bit rate is $R_Y = H(Y)$; after encoding, source X transmitted in an ideal channel and only in the decoding end can get side information Y as the "noise version" of X to help its decompression.

Obviously, Y can be regarded as the output of X after binary symmetric channel (Channel Binary Symmetrical, BSC) transmission, the correlated parameter P of X,Y can be viewed as transition probabilities of BSC. So the above problem can be described as follows: in order to correct the transmission errors of BSC under the conditions of the decoding end known as Y, what should the required minimum bit rate be? According to the Slepian–Wolf theory, the ideal lossless bit rate X can reach is:

$$R_{ideal} \geq H(X|Y) = H(P) = -P\log_2 P - (1 - P)\log_2(1 - P) \qquad (3.1)$$

Specifically speaking, the above question can be described as follows: verify the gap between the bit rate of adopted Slepian–Wolf encoder and the ideal value. The following introduction to Slepian–Wolf encoder mainly comes from the realization of algorithm and its performance evaluation.

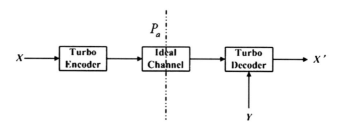

Fig. 3.3 Realization of Slepian–Wolf codec based on turbo code

3.3.2 Implementation Model

The implementation model of the Slepian–Wolf encoder based on turbo codes is
shown in Fig. 3.3. The coding end conducts turbo encoding for X and gets $Z = (X, P_a)$, where P_a is a parity bit. The coding end gives up the system bit X and
only transfers the parity bit P_a; the decoding end receives the parity bit P_a as well
as side information Y and inputs them into turbo decoder, then it conducts iterative
correction coding by using turbo codes and gets the restored X' (assuming that we
restore original value of X at a very small error probability).

3.3.3 The Encoding Algorithm

There are some differences between the coding algorithm of Slepian–Wolf based on
turbo codes and the traditional application algorithm; next, we will first introduce
the traditional process of coding and decoding of turbo, then we give the Slepian–
Wolf coding algorithm of turbo codes by comparison.

3.3.3.1 The Principles of Turbo Coding

As shown in Fig. 3.4, suppose the input data sequence is $D = (d_1, d_2, \ldots, d_N)$, it is
encoded in the first coding unit RSC1 (recursive systematic convolution) of turbo,
then we get the corresponding pariting sequence $C_1 = (c_{1,1}, c_{1,2}, c_{1,3}, \ldots, c_{1,N})$;
meanwhile $D = (d_1, d_2, \ldots, d_N)$ enters the second coding unit RSC2 via an inter-
leaver to code, and we get another parity sequence $C_2 = (c_{2,1}, c_{2,2}, c_{2,3}, \ldots, c_{2,N})$.
Multiplex the systematic information $D = (d_1, d_2, \ldots, d_N)$ and the parity sequence
after puncturing, in the end, we get the output sequence of turbo codes $S = (s_1, s_2, \ldots, s_N)$ in which $s_k = (d_k, c_k), d_k, c_k \in \{0, 1\}$.

In turbo decoding algorithm, assuming that the modulation mode is binary
phase shift keying (BPSK), then d_k and c_k are converted to symbols whose

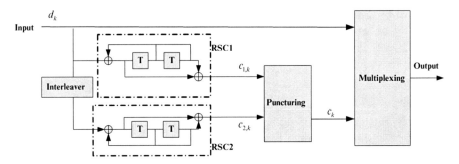

Fig. 3.4 Turbo encoder

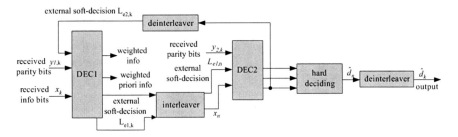

Fig. 3.5 Turbo decoder

values are ± 1 and, at the same time, assuming that the transmission channel is white Gaussian noise channel, modem uses the method of soft demodulation, then the input information of the decoder are $X = (x_1, x_2, \ldots, x_N)$ and $Y = (y_{1,1}, y_{2,1}, y_{1,2}, y_{2,2}, \ldots, y_{1,N}, y_{2,N})$, respectively, in which

$$x_k = (2d_k - 1) + \omega_{x,k}$$

$$y_{1,k} = (2c_{1,k} - 1) + \omega_{y_1,k}$$

$$y_{2,k} = (2c_{2,k} - 1) + \omega_{y_2,k} \tag{3.2}$$

where $\omega_{x,k}$, $\omega_{y_1,k}$, and $\omega_{y_2,k}$ are Gaussian random variables of independent identical distribution of zero mean, and the variance is σ^2. If the encoder output has been deleted, then when decoding, use 0 as an alternative of the deleted information. $x_k, y_{1,k}, y_{2,k}$ is input into the turbo decoder.

The turbo decoder is shown in Fig. 3.5, and the complete input information of the decoding unit DEC1 can be represented as $R_1^N = \{R_1, R_2, \ldots, R_N\}$, in which $R_k = (x_k, y_k, L_{e2,k})$, system bit x_k, parity sequence $y_{1,k}$, and the prior information delivered by DEC2, at the time when we conduct original decoding, $L_{e2,k}$ can be expressed as the logarithmic of the ratio of the prior probabilities of "1" and "0", that is,

$$L_{e2,k} = \log \frac{Pr(d_k = 1)}{Pr(d_k = 0)} \tag{3.3}$$

During the process of decoding, the main target of the algorithm is to calculate the logarithm-likelihood ratio based on the received code element sequence and prior information sequence when the input information bits d_k are 0 and 1, respectively:

$$\Lambda_1(d_k) = \log \frac{Pr(d_k = 1 | R_1^N)}{Pr(d_k = 0 | R_1^N)} \tag{3.4}$$

Here, $Pr(d_k = i | R_1^N), i = 0, 1$ is called coder acceptable codeword R_1^N, then we send a posteriori probability of $d_k = i$.

Assuming that the constraint length of RSC encoder is K, then the state of the encoder in moment K can be represented as

$$S_k = (a_k, a_{k-1}, \ldots, a_{k-K+1})$$

Here, $a_k \in \{0, 1\}$, at the same time assuming that the various information bit in information sequence bit are independent, the value is 0 or 1 at the same probability, and the initial state of the encoder S_0 and the end state S_N are both equal to zero, that is,

$$S_0 = S_N = (0, 0, \ldots, 0) \tag{3.5}$$

In this way, the posteriori probability of decoding bit d_k can be sought by the following joint probability:

$$Pr(d_k = i | R_1^N) = \sum_m Pr(d_k = i, S_k = m | R_1^N) = \sum_m \lambda_k^i(m) \tag{3.6}$$

So the following can be obtained:

$$\Lambda_1(d_k) = \log \frac{\sum_m \lambda_k^1(m)}{\sum_m \lambda_k^0(m)} \tag{3.7}$$

Because the events that occurred after moment k are not affected by observation R_1^k and input encoding information bitd_k, with Bayesian criterion, we can get

$$\Lambda_1(d_k) = \log \frac{\sum_m \sum_{m'} \Pr(d_k = 1, S_k = m, S_{k-1} = m', R_1^{k-1}, R_k, R_{k+1}^N)}{\sum_m \sum_{m'} \Pr(d_k = 0, S_k = m, S_{k-1} = m', R_1^{k-1}, R_k, R_{k+1}^N)}$$

$$= \log \frac{\sum_m \sum_{m'} \Pr(R_{k+1}^N/S_k = m) \Pr(S_{k-1} = m'/R_1^{k-1})}{\sum_m \sum_{m'} \Pr(R_{k+1}^N/S_k = m) \Pr(S_{k-1} = m'/R_1^{k-1})}$$

$$\cdot \frac{\Pr(d_k = 1, S_k = m, R_k/S_{k-1} = m')}{\Pr(d_k = 0, S_k = m, R_k/S_{k-1} = m')} \tag{3.8}$$

In order to calculate log-likelihood ratio of (3.8), we introduce the following probability functions:

$$\alpha_k(m) = \Pr(S_k = m/R_1^k) \tag{3.9}$$

$$\beta_k(m) = \frac{\Pr(R_{k+1}^N/S_k = m)}{\Pr(R_{k+1}^N/R_1^k)} \tag{3.10}$$

$$\gamma_i(R_k, m', m) = \Pr(d_k = i, S_k = m, R_k/S_{k-1} = m') \tag{3.11}$$

Then

$$\Lambda_1(d_k) = \log \frac{\sum_m \sum_{m'} \gamma_1(R_k, m', m)\alpha_{k-1}(m')\beta_k(m)}{\sum_m \sum_{m'} \gamma_0(R_k, m', m)\alpha_{k-1}(m')\beta_k(m)} \tag{3.12}$$

Here, the probability functions $\alpha_k(m)$ and $\beta_k(m)$ can be obtained by conducting recursive computation for $\gamma_i(R_k, m', m)$.

3.3.3.2 The Conclusion of Turbo Decoding Steps

Step 1: Initialization, initialize α and β; the prior information $L_{e2,k}$ of DEC1 should be initialized to 0.

$$\alpha_0(S) = \begin{cases} 1 & S = 0 \\ 0 & S \neq 0 \end{cases} \tag{3.13}$$

$$\beta_k(S) = \begin{cases} 1 & S = 0 \\ 0 & S \neq 0 \end{cases} \tag{3.14}$$

Step 2: For each observation $R_k = (x_k, y_{1,k}, L_{e2,k})$

$$\gamma_i(R_k, m', m) = p(x_k/d_k = i) \cdot p(y_{1,k}/d_k = i, S_k = m, S_{k-1} = m')$$
$$\cdot p(L_{e2,k}/d_k = i) \cdot \Pr(d_k = i, S_k = m/S_{k-1} = m') \tag{3.15}$$

Then use forward recursive arithmetic to find out:

$$\alpha_k(m) = \frac{\sum_{m'} \sum_{i=0}^{1} \alpha_{k-1}(m') \cdot \gamma_i(R_k, m', m)}{\sum_{m} \sum_{m'} \sum_{i=0}^{1} \alpha_{k-1}(m') \cdot \gamma_i(R_k, m', m)} \tag{3.16}$$

Step 3: When R_1^N are all received, calculate

$$\beta_k(m) = \frac{\sum_{m'} \sum_{i=0}^{1} \beta_{k+1}(m') \cdot \gamma_i(R_{k+1}, m', m)}{\sum_{m} \sum_{m'} \sum_{i=0}^{1} \alpha_k(m') \cdot \gamma_i(R_{k+1}, m', m)} \tag{3.17}$$

Step 4: Calculate the soft output information of DEC1

$$\Lambda_1(d_k) = \log \frac{\sum_{m} \sum_{m'} \gamma_1(R_k, m', m)\alpha_{k-1}(m')\beta_k(m)}{\sum_{m} \sum_{m'} \gamma_0(R_k, m', m)\alpha_{k-1}(m')\beta_k(m)} \tag{3.18}$$

Then calculate external information:

$$L_{e1,k} = \log \frac{\sum_{m} \sum_{m'} \gamma_1(R_k, m', m)\alpha_{k-1}(m')\beta_k(m)}{\sum_{m} \sum_{m'} \gamma_0(R_k, m', m)\alpha_{k-1}(m')\beta_k(m)} - \frac{2 \cdot x_k}{\sigma^2} - L_{e2,k} \tag{3.19}$$

Step 5: For decoding unit DEC2, the soft input information is $R_n = (x_n, y_{2,n}, L_{e1,n})$, then use the following formula to calculate soft output information of DEC2:

$$\Lambda_2(d_n) = \log \frac{\sum_{m} \sum_{m'} \gamma_1(R_n, m', m)\alpha_{n-1}(m')\beta_n(m)}{\sum_{m} \sum_{m'} \gamma_0(R_n, m', m)\alpha_{n-1}(m')\beta_n(m)} \tag{3.20}$$

The external information $L_{e2,n}$ is:

$$L_{e2,n} = \log \frac{\sum_{m} \sum_{m'} \gamma_1(R_n, m', m)\alpha_{n-1}(m')\beta_n(m)}{\sum_{m} \sum_{m'} \gamma_0(R_n, m', m)\alpha_{n-1}(m')\beta_n(m)} - \frac{2 \cdot x_n}{\sigma^2} - L_{e1,n} \tag{3.21}$$

Step 6: Repeated iteration.

Step 7: When the iterative decoding reaches the scheduled frequency, it will naturally terminate, then we judge the soft output information Λ_2 of DEC2, and we finally get the corrected information sequence after turbo code decoding.

$$\hat{d}_k = 1 \quad \text{if} \quad \Lambda_2(d_k) \geq 0$$
$$\hat{d}_k = 0 \quad \text{if} \quad \Lambda_2(d_k) < 0 \tag{3.22}$$

3.3.3.3 The Slepian–Wolf Codec Based on Turbo Codes

In Slepian–Wolf encoder based on turbo codes, the encoding algorithm and the traditional methods are the same, that is, as long as we turn the input information d in Fig. 3.4 to binary sequence X to encode, and the encoded output is recorded as (X, P_a). There are some changes in the decoding algorithm. Assume that the information bit X transmitted through the BSC and assuming that the parity bit P_a transmits without distortion, the changes of decoding algorithm appear as follows:

In step 1, $L_{e2,k}$ of DEC1 is initialized according to the side information because

$$p(x_k/d_k = i) = \begin{cases} 1 - P & (x_k = 0, \ i = 0) \\ P & (x_k = 1, \ i = 0) \\ 1 - P & (x_k = 1, \ i = 1) \\ P & (x_k = 0, \ i = 1) \end{cases} \tag{3.23}$$

So, if the side information is 1, then $L_{e2,k}$ is initialized as:

$$L_{e2,k} = \log\left(\frac{1-P}{P}\right) \tag{3.24}$$

If side information is 0, then $L_{e2,k}$ is initialized as:

$$L_{e2,k} = \log\left(\frac{P}{1-P}\right) \tag{3.25}$$

In step 2, the transition probability is $\gamma_i(R_k, m', m)$ using Formula 3.15.

In step 4 and step 5, we use the statistical parameters of BSC channel to calculate $L_{e1,k}$, $L_{e2,n}$.

3.3.4 RCPT Codec Principles

In turbo Slepian–Wolf coding, we assume that the decoding side receives enough parity bits and so it realizes turbo decoding successfully. But in fact, in Slepian–Wolf

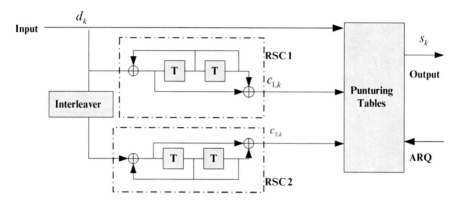

Fig. 3.6 RCPT encoder

coding, the coding side does not know the correlation between the primary information and side information, so the encoding side does not know how many parity bits
it needs to make decoding successful, in particular, if the correlation of the main
information and side information does not change along with time, then it requires a
different number of parity bits which require the Slepian–Wolf encoder of different
rate to adapt to the changes in correlation while the turbo codes of fixed rate cannot
meet this requirement. In this case, we adopt turbo code in Slepian–Wolf coding
which is rate compatible, namely the RCPT (rate compatible punctured turbo) as
shown in Fig. 3.6. RCPT means that turbo codes adopt a generated matrix, but you
can get multiple bit rate by deleting; any one of a higher bit rate can be obtained by
increasing some bits on the basis of low bit rate, that is, low bit rate is contained in
high bit rate, and bit transmitted in low bit rate is a component of high bit rate.

Constructing the puncturing matrix which is bit rate compatible is the key of
RCPT code. For example, for parent code with bit rate $R = 1/2$, we can get the
codeword of different bit rate through different punch table. The following is a four-
level puncturing table in which 1 means that the output of the corresponding location
is preserved, 0 means that it is deleted:

$$
A(1) = \begin{bmatrix} 1 & 1 & 1 & 0 \\ 1 & 0 & 0 & 1 \end{bmatrix} \qquad
A(2) = \begin{bmatrix} 1 & 1 & 1 & 0 \\ 1 & 1 & 0 & 1 \end{bmatrix}
$$

$$
A(3) = \begin{bmatrix} 1 & 1 & 1 & 1 \\ 1 & 1 & 0 & 1 \end{bmatrix} \qquad
A(4) = \begin{bmatrix} 1 & 1 & 1 & 1 \\ 1 & 1 & 1 & 1 \end{bmatrix}
\tag{3.26}
$$

The bit rates are 5/4, 4, 6/7/4, and 8/4, respectively. These punch codes are
compatible in bit rate, as can be seen from one table $A(m_1)$. If the value of a_{ij}
is 1, then in any table $A(m_2), m_2 > m_1$, its value must be 1. The receiving end will

accord to the rule of deleting to conduct interpolation for the received sequence and add an intermediate value at the deleted data bit (such as 0).

In the traditional puncturing algorithm of RCPT, the information bits and parity bits have both been deleted, and the encoding based on RCPT Slepian–Wolf only pass parity bit, so it is only on the parity bit for puncturing.

3.3.5 Experimental Results and Analysis

In this section, we will verify the compression performance of the RCPT-based Slepian–Wolf encoder. The original rate systematic turbo codes is 1/3. That is, input n information bits, we can get $3n$ bits through the encoder; the information bits are ahead of the parity bits; the generated matrix $g = [37, 11]$, and the puncturing matrix uses Formula 3.27 and adopts a pseudo random interleaved mode; the number of decoding iteration is 10, and we regard it as correct decoding when bit code rate $P_e \leq 10^{-5}$. The specific steps are as follows:

1. Input source X and get $3n$ bits, remove the information bits X and store the parity bit P_a in the cache
2. Adjust the rate according to the puncturing matrix and ARQ feedback information. Here, the adopted bit rate $1/8, 2/8, \ldots 7/8, 1$, as shown in Formulas 3.2–3.26 is the puncturing matrix.

$$
A(1) = \begin{bmatrix} 00000000 \\ 00000001 \\ 00000000 \end{bmatrix}, \quad
A(2) = \begin{bmatrix} 00000000 \\ 00000001 \\ 00000001 \end{bmatrix}, \quad
A(3) = \begin{bmatrix} 00000000 \\ 10000001 \\ 00000001 \end{bmatrix},
$$

$$
A(4) = \begin{bmatrix} 00000000 \\ 10000001 \\ 10000001 \end{bmatrix}
A(5) = \begin{bmatrix} 00000000 \\ 10001001 \\ 10000001 \end{bmatrix}, \quad
A(6) = \begin{bmatrix} 00000000 \\ 10010001 \\ 10010001 \end{bmatrix},
$$

$$
A(7) = \begin{bmatrix} 00000000 \\ 10011001 \\ 10010001 \end{bmatrix}, \quad
A(8) = \begin{bmatrix} 00000000 \\ 10011001 \\ 10011001 \end{bmatrix} \tag{3.27}
$$

3. When it is initialized, the lowest transmission bit rate is 1/8; if the receiving end is not able to decode correctly, then conduct decoding after supplementing 1/8 bit from the cache according to the puncturing matrix rules of RCPT transport.
4. Combine the parity bit with side information Y, and then, we get $\hat{Z} = (Y, C)$; the drilled bit is set to 0.

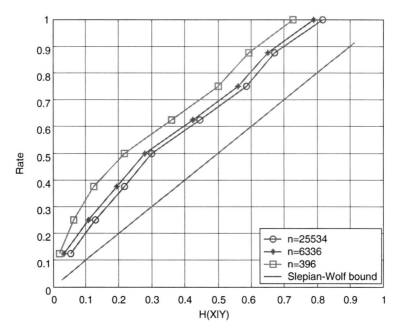

Fig. 3.7 Rate curves of Slepian–Wolf codec based on turbo coding

5. Do joint decoding; we get the corresponding X' from $\hat{Z}$ after turbo encoder. If X' meets the requirements of rate distortion or it reaches the maximum number of iterations, finish the encoding and give the present used bit rate, otherwise go back to step 3.

Figure 3.7 shows that when X and Y are under different correlations, the performance curve of the Slepian–Wolf encoder is based on RCPT code, and compare it with the ideal limit value $H(X|Y) = H(P) = -P\log_2 P - (1 - P)\log_2(1 - P)$, P is the cross-transition probability. As can be seen from the figure, RCPT can realize bit rate adaptive; it has a better compression effect when the transition probability P is low; the gap with the ideal value is about 0.1 dB. But when the correlation is poor (when P is large) and the gap with ideal boundary value reaches more than 0.2 dB, for example, when $P > 0.2$, we can only use $R_X = H(X) = 1$ restore X, almost no compression performance; the reason is that drill based on the parity bit has a great impact on the performance of turbo. The Slepian–Wolf encoder with higher performance requires improvement from the structure of turbo codes; in addition, the experiment shows that with the increasing of the input sequence length, due to the fact that the capacity to correct is stronger when the turbo sequence is long, the performance of Slepian–Wolf is closer to the Slepian–Wolf limit.

3.4 LDPC-Based Slepian–Wolf Coding

The performance of low-density parity codes (LDPC) [5–7] is better than the turbo codes when the mid-long code is long, and it also has the characteristic of lower decoding complexity; parallel decoding and coding errors can be detected, etc., and it has become the hotspot of channel coding. The performance of Slepian–Wolf encoder based on LDPC is better than the turbo codes [8, 9], so most of the present Slepian–Wolf encoders use LDPC codes. This section first describes coding theory of LDPC, the coding algorithm of Slepian–Wolf based on LDPC, then describes the bit rate adaptive LDPCA (low-density parity codes accumulate) code proposed by Varodayan et al. [10]; finally, the simulation gives the performance comparison of Slepian–Wolf encoder-based LDPCA.

3.4.1 The Coding Theory of LDPC

Low-density parity codes are essentially linear block codes, the coding through a generated matrix G to map the information $s = \{s_1, s_2, \ldots, s_m\}$ to the codeword to be sent $t = \{t_1, t_2, \ldots, t_k\}$, that is, $t = s \times G$. For the generated matrix G, there is a corresponding parity–parity matrix $H_{(k-m) \times k}$, where H meets the conditions $H \times t^T = 0$ and $G \times H^T = 0$.

The decoding of LDPC adopts the algorithm of iterative probability decoding of belief propagation [9]. Assume the received information is $r = t + n$, where n is the noise, then $z = Hr^T = HG^Ts^T + Hn^T = Hn^T$. In the process of decoding, according to the parity matrix H, we can obtain a corresponding bidirectional map; the node in the diagram is divided into two groups: one group represents noise signal, and the other represents the parity information, represented by the node sequence $x = \{x_1, x_2, \ldots, x_k\}$ and $z = \{z_1, z_2, \ldots, z_m\}$, respectively. In parity matrix H, if H_{ij} does not equal to 0, nodes z_i and x_j of bipartite graph are connected. The adjacent node of noise node x_j is called child node, the adjacent node of parity node z_i is called its father node; according to the information received and the given characteristics of channel, in each step of the decoding process, we can estimate the posteriori of each noise signal; decoding is to find the estimate value x of noise signal n to make $Hx^T = z$.

During the decoding process of BP, the node x_j sends information Q_{ij}^b to each of its child nodes z_i; it is to inform z_i the probability of node x_j in state b, the value Q_{ij}^b to be sent to node z_i is interrelated to all the child nodes of x_j, except z_i. Similarly, node z_i also sends R_{ij}^b which represents the status of b to its corresponding node; the value R_{ij}^b sent to node x_j is related to the child nodes of z_i, except x_j. Decoding process is an iterative algorithm. Each iteration will update the value of R_{ij}^b and Q_{ij}^b, and on the basis of the updated value of R_{ij}^b and Q_{ij}^b, it will produce a temporary decoding value. Iteration operations will continue until the temporary value meets the equation $Hx^T = z$, or the number of iterations reaches the maximum number of iterations (the current experience of iteration is 200 times). If the decoding values meet the equation $Hx^T = z$, the decoding is successful; if it still cannot satisfy the equation $Hx^T = z$ when the number of iterations reaches to the limit, then the decoding fails.

3.4.2 The Implementation of LDPC Slepian–Wolf Encoder

LDPC Slepian–Wolf encoder based on the syndrome encoding, the specific encoding algorithm involves the following steps:

1. Let the input sequence X be multiplied by the parity matrix H, and the result is the syndrome S, $S = X \times H^T$.
2. Send the syndrome S to the decoding end.

The syndrome S is received in the decoding end, and side information Y uses BP algorithm of the modified version to find out X; the specific modification appears in the following:

- When the syndrome equals to zero, which indicates that the input codeword can be directly decoded by the traditional method of BP.
- If the associated type does not equal to zero (all nonzero syndromes are marked on the corresponding parity nodes in the diagram), then we change the output symbol of the parity node and then apply the BP algorithm. This is because the inverse verification and inverse operation in log-domain mean sign change to the parity nodes [10].

3.4.3 The Coding and Decoding Algorithms of LDPCA Slepian–Wolf

Similar to turbo code, conducting puncturing and deleting for the syndrome after LDPC Slepian–Wolf encoding in last section can also achieve adjustable bit rate for Slepian–Wolf, but its performance is poor when the rate of compression is high because the figure of LDPC structure includes noise node which is disconnected or single connected [10]; these structures prevent the exchange of information in BP iterative decoding algorithm. Therefore, Varodayan et al. [10] suggest that we should use bit rate adaptive LDPCA to improve its performance; next, we will introduce this method.

3.4.3.1 Encoding Algorithm

Figure 3.8 represents a coding structure of LDPCA; its encoding end consists of an accumulator and an LDPC syndrome generator. First, according to the graph

Fig. 3.8 LDPCA encoder
[10]

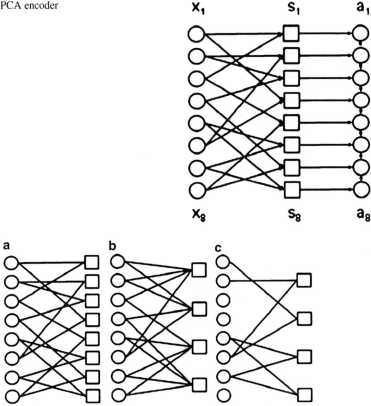

Fig. 3.9 LDPCA decoder [10]

structure of LDPC, the syndrome does syndrome operations on the input node on the input source bit $X = (x_1, x_2, \ldots, x_8) S = X \times H^T$, creates syndrome bit $S = (s_1, s_2, \ldots, s_8)$, then conduct continuous modulo-2 addition for every syndrome component, and generates cumulative syndrome $S = (s_1, s_2, \ldots, s_8)$; the encoding end stores the cumulative syndrome temporarily and then transmits it to the decoding end step by step.

3.4.3.2 Decoding Algorithm

Every time the LDPCA decoder receives the newly sent cumulative syndrome, by modifying its decoding graph to achieve rate adaptation. To facilitate discussions, first of all, assume that all of the cumulative syndrome $(a_1, a_2, \ldots, a_8)$ is received, as shown in Figs. 3.2–3.9. For decoding algorithm, noise node is assigned to the conditional probability $\Pr\{x_1|Y\}, \ldots, \Pr\{x_8|Y\}$ of the given side information, then the information is delivered back and forth between the noise node and parity node

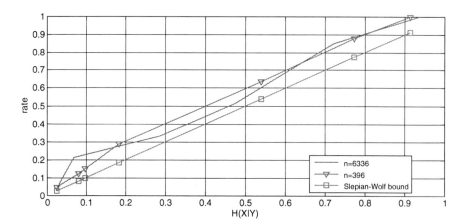

Fig. 3.10 Rate curves of Slepian–Wolf codec based on LDPCA

until the estimation of noise bit is convergent. The restored value of the source is correct or not can be judged by the syndrome bit, as mentioned above. In this case, when the number of received bits is equal to the number of bits of information source, the performance of through the delivery of $(s_1, s_2, \ldots, s_8)$ has no difference with the direct delivery of $(a_1, a_2, \ldots, a_8)$.

Modifications to the decoding graph appear when the compression rate is high. For example, consider the compression ratio is 2, which equivalents to only transmit the cumulative syndrome of the even index (a_2, a_4, a_6, a_8). Continuous modula-2 difference then produces $(s_1 + s_2, s_3 + s_4, s_5 + s_6, s_7 + s_8)$. Figure 3.9b demonstrates the encoding graph from $(x_1, x_2, \ldots, x_8)$ to $(s_1 + s_2, s_3 + s_4, s_5 + s_6, s_7 + s_8)$; this figure preserves all the information of the noise node same as Fig. 3.9a so that when the source is assigned in the conditional probability $\Pr\{x_1|Y\}, \ldots, \Pr\{x_8|Y\}$, it can be applied in an effective iterative decoding; at this point, when the source decoding is finished, the restored source can use the syndrome to verify its accuracy. For the sake of comparison, Fig. 3.9c shows the decoding graph when we only receive the even syndrome (s_2, s_4, s_6, s_8) instead of receiving the subset of cumulative syndrome (a_2, a_4, a_6, a_8) from which we can see that the quality declines seriously and is not good for iterative algorithm.

Finally, note that coding and decoding the complexity of LDPCA is $o(n)$ in which n is the bit length of coding block.

3.4.4 Experimental Results and Analysis

According to the source code provided by Stanford (http://ivms.stanford.edu/~dsc/wzcodingvideo), we test the compression performance of LDPCA of two different lengths which are $n = 396$ and $n = 6,336$, respectively, as can be seen from

Figs. 3.2–3.10; the difference between the limit of Slepian–Wolf and LDPCA is 0.03–0.1 dB for shorter code length $n = 396$; when the correlation is high ($H(X|Y) < 0.18$.), the performance of LDPCA is also very good.

3.5 Summary

This chapter introduced the basic principle of the DSC coding from the perspective of error-correcting codes. We illustrated the implementation of DSC coding by providing the coding and decoding algorithm of Slepian–Wolf encoder based on turbo code and LDPC code and tested their performance in binary source compression.

References

1. Slepian, D., Wolf, J.K.: Noiseless coding of correlated information sources. IEEE Trans. Inf. Theory 19(4), 471–480 (1973)
2. Wyner, A., Ziv, J.: The rate-distortion function for source coding with side information at the decoder. IEEE Trans. Inf. Theory 22(1), 1–10 (1976)
3. Zamir, R.: The rate loss in the Wyner-Ziv problem. IEEE Trans. Inf. Theory 42(6), 2073–2084 (1996)
4. Griod, B., Aaron, A., Rane, S.: Distributed video coding. Proc. IEEE 93(1), 71–83 (2005)
5. Gallager, R.G.: Low density parity codes. IEEE Trans. Inf. Theory IT-8, 21–28 (1962)
6. Richardsom, T., Urbanke, R.: Efficient encoding of low-density parity-parity codes. IEEE Trans. Inf. Theory 47(2), 638–656 (2001)
7. Davey, M.C., MacKay, D.J.C.: Low density parity-parity codes over GF (q). IEEE Commun. Lett. 2, 165–167 (1998)
8. Schonberg, D., Pradhan, S.S., Ramchandran, K.: LDPC codes can approach the Slepian-Wolf bound for general binary sources. In: Proceedings of Allerton Conference on Communication, Control, and Computing, Allerton, IL (2002)
9. Leveris, A., Xiong, Z., Geolrghiades, C.: Compression of binary sources with side information at the decoder using LDPC codes. IEEE Commun. Lett. 6(10), 440–442 (2002)
10. Varodayan, D., Aaron, A., Girod, B.: Rate-adaptive distributed source coding using low-density parity-check codes. In: Proceedings of Asilomar Conference on Signals, Systems and Computers, Pacific Grove, pp. 1–8 (2005)

Chapter 4
Algorithms of MD

Network congestion and delay sensibility pose great challenges for multimedia communication system design. This creates a need for coding approaches combining high compression efficiency and robustness. Multiple-description (MD) coding has emerged as an attractive framework for robust transmission over unreliable channels. It can effectively combat packet loss without any retransmission, thus satisfying the demand of real-time services and relieving the network congestion [1]. Multiple-description coding encodes the source message into several bit streams (descriptions) carrying different information, which can then be transmitted over separate channels. If only one channel works, only one description can be individually decoded to guarantee a minimum fidelity in the reconstruction at the receiver. When more channels work, the descriptions from these channels can be combined to yield a higher fidelity reconstruction.

In recent years, our research group has proposed some novel schemes of MD for image and video transmission, which have shown promising results compared with the conventional schemes.

4.1 Optimized MDLVQ for Wavelet Image

4.1.1 Motivation

The MD versions of transforms [2] and quantizers [3–8] are the two main techniques for the design of MD image coding. An MD image coder using pair-wise correlation transform is presented in [2]. A design of multiple-description scalar quantizers (MDSQ) for image coding is described in [3], which exploits a suboptimal algorithm to allocate rate subject to global constraints on the coding bit rate and side distortion. In [5], an MD image coding algorithm is developed also based on MDSQ with optimization of MDSQ parameters, which produces similar PSNR values with about 50–60% of the bit rates required by the two above-mentioned MD image coders.

H. Bai et al., *Distributed Multiple Description Coding*,
DOI 10.1007/978-1-4471-2248-7_4, © Springer-Verlag London Limited 2011

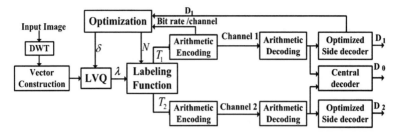

Fig. 4.1 Block diagram of our proposed scheme

In [6], a modified MDSQ (MMDSQ) is designed in two stages, that is, the first stage is a basic MDSQ stage, while the second stage is a finer central quantizer to quantize the residuals from the first one. The MMDSQ is applied to the Tarp filter image coder with classification for embedding (TCE) [9], which is reported to have achieved better performance. In addition, to be compatible with the image coding standards, some other methods, like that in [10], have designed MD image coders without using any special transforms or MD quantizers. In contrast, the MD coding scheme in [10] directly utilizes streams produced by a JPEG2000 encoder and exploits the rate allocation of JPEG2000 streams to produce MD streams.

We attempt to apply MD lattice vector quantization (MDLVQ) for the design of a more effective two-channel MD (or two-description) image coder. In this part, some effective enhancements are considered to substantially improve the performance of MDLVQ-based image coding. Several factors which are important and of significant impact to the performance are taken into consideration for optimized MDLVQ encoding and decoding. Firstly, the forming of coefficient vectors needs to adapt to different correlating characteristics between wavelet coefficients in different sub-bands. Secondly, like the optimization for the MD scalar quantization (MDSQ) [5], the MDLVQ encoding parameters need to be optimized in terms of rate-distortion performance in view of the varying importance of different sub-bands. More importantly, the construction quality from the conventional MDLVQ side decoders can be significantly improved by utilizing inter-vector correlation and predicting the lost information when necessary for further reducing the side distortion. To realize the optimized side decoding, an alternative transmission of MDLVQ labels is developed.

4.1.2 Overview

Figure 4.1 illustrates our scheme, and a step-by-step recipe is explained as follows. Here, we consider two balance channels, that is, the bit rate of two descriptions and the side distortions for the two side decoders are approximately the same.

Fig. 4.2 Vector construction
in different sub-bands

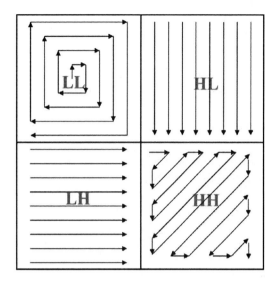

Step 1: Wavelet Decomposition

A given input image is decomposed into sub-bands (sub-band 1, sub-band 2...,
sub-band m, denoted by s_i, $i = 1, 2, \ldots, m$), by applying a wavelet transform.
Following that done in [5], small wavelet coefficients are set to zeros by applying
an appropriate threshold.

Step 2: Vector Construction

After wavelet decomposition, correlation still remains between coefficients in
the sub-bands. Grouping the coefficients appropriately can exploit intra-vector
redundancy well. During wavelet decomposition, sub-bands arise from separa-
ble application of vertical and horizontal filters, denoted as LL, HL, LH, HH,
respectively [11]. It is known that wavelet coefficients in different sub-bands
have different directional correlations. For example, vertical correlation exhibits
in HL coefficients, horizontal correlation in LH, diagonal correlation in HH, and
neighboring correlation of low-frequency components in LL. Therefore, it is more
efficient to group coefficients in different sub-bands according to their directional
correlation. Figure 4.2 shows our scheme for vector construction: HL is scanned
to form vectors along vertical direction, LH is scanned in horizontal direction, and
HH is scanned in zigzag way. In addition, spiral scan is also applied in LL sub-band
considering the strong correlation among neighboring coefficients. Predictive vector
quantization can be applied to further exploit these correlations.

Step 3: Lattice Vector Quantizer (LVQ)

In this chapter, lattice A_2 is used for lattice vector quantization (LVQ). It has
been shown [4] that in the two-channel case, MDLVQ using A_2 exhibits better

performance than that based on Z_2 in terms of central and side distortions. A_2 is equivalent or similar to the hexagonal lattice [12]. The hexagonal lattice can be spanned by the vectors $(1, 0)$ and $(-1/2, \sqrt{3}/2)$, and the generator matrix is

$$G = \begin{bmatrix} 1 & 0 \\ -\dfrac{1}{2} & \dfrac{\sqrt{3}}{2} \end{bmatrix}. \tag{4.1}$$

Every pair of coefficients in each subband is formed as a two-dimensional vector according to the grouping way in step 2. A lattice vector quantizer with a quantization "volume-size" (like the step-size in scalar quantization) is applied to such two-dimensional vectors, thus producing a quantized symbol λ, $\lambda \subset A_2$. It is known that the VQ encoding complexity increases with dimensionality and codebook size. Here we use the lowest dimension vector, that is, two-dimensional vector. Moreover, LVQ encoding can be implemented by a fast quantizing algorithm [12] which does not require performing the computation-intensive nearest neighbor search based on squared distance calculation. In the fast encoding algorithm [12], only two matrix multiplications are required for vector mapping between a two-dimensional vector and a three-dimensional vector, and a modification may be needed for the mapped three-dimensional vector to make the sum of its three-dimensional values zero. In this way, the complexity of LVQ on A_2 is considered very low. In addition, another fast quantizing algorithm in [12] may be a better choice to accelerate LVQ encoding further. Considering that the hexagonal lattice is the union of two rectangular lattices, the encoding can be simply achieved by finding the nearest point in each rectangular sub-lattice and selecting the nearer of these two points.

Step 4: Labeling Function with Alternative Transmission

Information about a quantized point λ is mapped to two representations and then sent across two channels, subjected to bit rate constraints imposed by each individual channel. This is done by a labeling function [7] followed by arithmetic encoding. The labeling function maps $\lambda \subset \Lambda$ to a pair $(\lambda_1', \lambda_2') \in \Lambda' \times \Lambda'$, where Λ' is a sub-lattice of Λ with the index N, $N = |\Lambda/\Lambda'|$. The index N determines the coarse degree of the sub-lattice which can control the amount of redundancy in the MD coder [4]. In Sect. 4.1.3, optimization for the index N and the LVQ quantization "volume-size" (in step 3) will be presented in detail.

Figure 4.3 is an example of an A_2 sub-lattice with index $N = 13$. In the case of $N = 13$, we can obtain a labeling function as in Table 4.1, where each fine lattice point λ is mapped to a unique label (λ_1', λ_2'), with λ_1' and λ_2' being two sub-lattice points as close to λ as possible. Note that the proposed mapping scheme shown in the table is slightly different from the index assignment developed by Servetto, Vaishampayan, and Sloane [4] (known as SVS technique). In our proposed scheme, λ_1' is always closer to λ, thus λ_1' is denoted as the near sub-lattice point and λ_2' the

Fig. 4.3 Example of sub-lattice with index 13: fine lattice points are labeled by $a, b, c, \ldots, l$, and sub-lattice points are $A, B, C, \ldots, F$

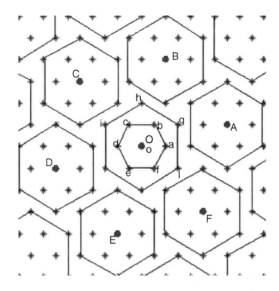

Table 4.1 Labeling function with $N = 13$

Lattice point λ	Label	Lattice point λ	Label
o	(O,O)		
a	(O,A)	d	(O,D)
b	(O,B)	e	(O,E)
f	(O,F)	c	(O,C)
g	(B,F)	j	(E,C)
h	(C,A)	k	(F,D)
i	(D,B)	l	(A,E)

far sub-lattice point. To strike a balance of reconstruction quality with any single-description sequence, λ'_1 and λ'_2 are alternately transmitted over two channels.

As a simple example, if we have a quantized sequence of fine lattice points $\{\lambda(1), \lambda(2), \ldots, \lambda(8)\} = \{a, a, a, b, b, b, i, i\}$, then the two sequences of sub-lattice points using the labeling function in Table 4.1 are $\{\lambda'_1(1), \lambda'_1(2), \ldots, \lambda'_1(8)\} = \{O, O, O, O, O, O, D, D\}$ and $\{\lambda'_2(1), \lambda'_2(2), \ldots, \lambda'_2(8)\} = \{A, A, A, B, B, B, B, B\}$. Based on the alternative transmission scheme, the sequence

$$T_1 = \{\lambda'_1(1), \lambda'_2(2), \lambda'_1(3), \lambda'_2(4), \ldots, \lambda'_1(7), \lambda'_2(8)\} = \{O, A, O, B, O, B, D, B\}$$

is transmitted over channel 1 and

$$T_2 = \{\lambda'_1(1), \lambda'_2(2), \lambda'_1(3), \lambda'_2(4), \ldots, \lambda'_1(7), \lambda'_2(8)\} = \{A, O, A, O, B, O, B, D\}$$

over channel 2. The alternative transmission way is exploited in predicting lost description in the optimized side decoding, which will be explained in Sect. 4.1.3.2.

A general and widely used context-based arithmetic codec [13] is applied to code the sequences of $\{T_1\}$ and $\{T_2\}$ before transmission. The arithmetic coding used in our scheme is based on a three-order "finite-context" model, that is, three previous symbols make up the context.

Step 5: Central Decoder and Side Decoder

At the receiver, if both descriptions are received, the two descriptions can be processed by the central decoder after arithmetic decoding, and the sequence of fine lattice points $\{\lambda\}$ can be reconstructed with the central distortion. However, if either of the descriptions is lost, the conventional side decoder can only produce λ'_1 or λ'_2 as an approximate to λ, leading to a larger side distortion. In contrast, we can obtain a better side decoding result by performing lost information prediction when necessary, based on the neighboring inter-vector correlation of wavelet coefficients and the above-mentioned alternative transmission scheme. The design of the optimized side decoder with prediction will be elaborated in Sect. 4.1.3.

4.1.3 Encoding and Decoding Optimization

4.1.3.1 Encoding Parameter Optimization

In MDLVQ image encoding, there are two important factors which will affect the reconstruction image quality and the bit rate. The first one is the area of hexagonal lattice (in step 3), that is, the quantization "volume-size" used in LVQ, while the other is the choice of sub-lattice index (in step 4).

Since the lattice A_2 is the space which can be spanned by two vectors $(1, 0)$ and $(-1/2, \sqrt{3}/2)$, the area of the hexagonal lattice is determined by the two vectors. However, we can keep the shape of the hexagonal lattice and change its area by multiplying the generator matrix G by a factor $\delta (\delta \in R, \delta > 0)$. The parameter δ in the LVQ is similar to the step-size in scalar quantization (SQ). By changing δ, the central distortion D_0 and its associated bit rate can be adjusted.

For the lattice A_2, the choice of index N will not change the central distortion D_0 for a given δ. However, the side distortion D_1 and D_2 will be sensitive to the value of N. When the index N increases, D_0 has no change, but D_1 and D_2 will increase significantly. On the other hand, the bit rates associated with D_1 and D_2 will decrease with the increase of N. The index N is analogous to the number of diagonal of index assignment in MDSQ [5]. In MDSQ, the increasing of the number of diagonals will have severe impact on D_1 and D_2 and their associated rates, while D_0 does not change. It is desired to find the optimal parameters δ and N for striking the best trade-off among central distortion, side distortion, and their associated bit rates. With the analysis of analogies between MDLVQ and MDSQ, we can perform the optimization of parameters δ and N in MDLVQ encoding like the optimization way for MDSQ encoding in [5]. Therefore, we can formulate the MD design problem as yielding optimal performance in the presence of the constraints

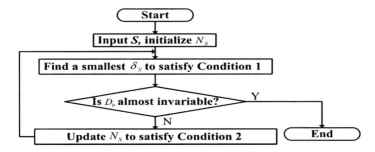

Fig. 4.4 The encoding optimization process

of the side distortion and its bit rate. To facilitate the description, some notations are defined in the following.

Let I denotes an image, and $S = \{s_1, s_2, \ldots, s_m\}$ its m wavelet sub-bands after the decomposition. δ_S refers to the magnified degree of the lattice area (i.e., quantization "volume-size") used for all the sub-bands. $N_S = \{N_{s_i} | i = 1, 2, \ldots, m\}$ represents the set of the index numbers used in the labeling function for different sub-bands. $D_0(S, \delta_S, N_S)$, $D_1(S, \delta_S, N_S)$, and $D_2(S, \delta_S, N_S)$ denote the mean squared errors (MSE) from the central decoder and the side decoders for the input image I, respectively, given the lattice vector quantizers with parameter δ_S and the index set $N_S \cdot R_1(S, \delta_S, N_S) . R_1(S, \delta_S, N_S)$ and $R_2(S, \delta_S, N_S)$ are the bit rates for encoding each description of I, respectively.

Our goal is to find the optimal parameters δ_S and N_S in solving the following optimization problem:

$$\min_{\delta_S, N_S} D_0(S, \delta_S, N_S) \tag{4.2}$$

subject to

$$\text{Condition 1:} \quad R_1(S, \delta_S, N_S) = R_2(S, \delta_S, N_S) = R_{\text{budget}} \tag{4.3}$$

$$\text{Condition 2:} \quad D_1(S, \delta_S, N_S) = D_2(S, \delta_S, N_S) = D_{\text{budget}} \tag{4.4}$$

where R_{budget} is the available bit rate to encode each description, and D_{budget} is the maximum distortion acceptable for single-channel reconstruction. The encoding optimization module in Fig. 4.1 is based on the above functions. With the constraints on the bit rate per channel and the side distortion, δ_S and N_S are adjusted accordingly to minimize the central distortion.

The optimization for the problem is carried out in an iterative way. The basic algorithm shown in Fig. 4.4 is to make use of the monotonicity of both R and D as the functions of δ_S. Firstly, after initialization a smallest δ_S is searched to minimize subject to Condition 1. Secondly, according to Condition 2, we can update

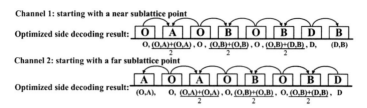

Fig. 4.5 Side decoding with prediction for better reconstruction: an example

N_S sequentially from high-frequency sub-bands to low ones. Then, the updated N_S affects $R_1(S, \delta_S, N_S)$ and $R_2(S, \delta_S, N_S)$ in Condition 1, and in turn δ_S will be updated to minimize D_0 further. So the two steps will be iterated to update δ_S and N_S until D_0 has little change.

4.1.3.2 Side Decoding Optimization with Prediction

At the receiver, when only one channel works, the normal side decoder just uses the received description as the reconstruction. However, in our scheme, we know that far sub-lattice points received may produce much larger side distortions than the near ones. Therefore, it is not advisable to reconstruct the value λ using the far sub-lattice point λ_2'. Considering that we only use two-dimensional vectors based on A_2 lattice, the correlation among wavelet coefficients is far from being exploited, especially those in the low-frequency sub-bands. We may consider exploiting inter-vector correlation to improve the reconstruction quality by predicting the lost near sub-lattice points. Given our alternative transmission way, the lost near sub-lattice point for the received far sub-lattice point can be bidirectionally predicted from the two neighboring (the previous and the following) near sub-lattice points received in the same description. If the received far sub-lattice point can form a valid label (pair) with its predicted near sub-lattice point (the previous or the following), then a fine lattice point can be reconstructed as a forward or backward approximate value. However, if the label obtained by the combination of the predicted near sub-lattice point with the received far sub-lattice point is not valid, the forward or backward approximate value of λ is the far sub-lattice point itself. The final reconstruction value from the side decoding is the average of forward and backward approximate values. It is noted that the prediction is performed for neighboring vectors in the same sub-band according to the directional correlation illustrated in Fig. 4.2. Another point to be noted is that the first or last sub-lattice point in a description has only backward or forward approximate value based on backward or forward prediction.

As an example, suppose channel 1 transmits the sequence of sub-lattice points starting with a near sub-lattice point and then followed by far and near sub-lattice points alternatively. Then, channel 2 starts with a far sub-lattice point. As shown in Fig. 4.5, if only channel 1 works with the received sequence $\{O, A, O, B, O, B, D,$

Table 4.2 Side PSNR values of normal scheme vs. optimized decoding scheme

Lena		$N = 7$	$N = 13$	$N = 19$	$N = 31$
Normal (dB)	Side 1	35.621	31.357	28.686	25.521
	Side 2	35.583	31.331	28.456	25.528
Optimized (dB)	Side 1	37.656	33.890	31.272	28.237
	Side 2	37.660	33.868	31.251	28.211
Barbara		$N = 7$	$N = 13$	$N = 19$	$N = 31$
Normal (dB)	Side 1	35.797	31.248	28.393	24.844
	Side 2	35.784	31.256	28.105	24.836
Optimized (dB)	Side 1	37.161	32.831	29.999	26.627
	Side 2	37.175	32.846	29.998	26.643

B}, based on our optimized side decoding with prediction, the reconstruction result is $\{O, a, O, b, O,$ midpoint of b and $i, D, i\}$. Similarly, if only $\{A, O, A, O, B, O, B, D\}$ is received from channel 2, $\{a, O, a, O, b, O,$ midpoint of b and $i, D\}$ is obtained as the reconstruction result. In fact, instead of directly using the near sub-lattice point as the reconstruction, one can also estimate the lost far sub-lattice point based on the same prediction rule, thus producing a likely better reconstruction by combining the received near sub-lattice point with the predicted far lattice point. However, a wrong prediction may lead to poorer reconstruction.

To substantiate the improvement of the proposed optimized side decoding over the normal side decoding, the following experiment was performed. Two standard images Lena (512 × 512) and Barbara (512 × 512) were directly encoded using MDLVQ with volume-size $\delta_S = 5$ and various index numbers. Then, they are decoded by the normal and the optimized side decoding, respectively. Table 4.2 shows that with the same bit rate and same central PSNR values, the side PSNR values by the optimized side decoding scheme are much higher than using the normal side decoding. Moreover, the difference between side PSNR values from two channels with our proposed scheme is around 0.03 dB, which shows that a balance of reconstruction quality is also maintained.

With these encoding and decoding optimization schemes, the overall performance of our MDLVQ has improved substantially, especially the side distortion results, as shown above. Inevitably computational complexity has also increased. The most time-consuming part is the encoding optimization which involves the iterative processing for finding the two encoding parameters. The decoding optimization only requires some more table lookup operations for fine lattice point location and simple averaging calculations, the computational cost of which is negligible. In view that the similar encoding optimization for two encoding parameters is also employed in the optimized MDSQ scheme in [5], the computational complexity of the optimization schemes in our MDLVQ is almost the same as that of the optimized MDSQ scheme.

Table 4.3 Results of optimized parameters for "Barbara"

δ_S	N_S					Central PSNR (dB)	Side PSNR (dB)
18.125	7,	7,7,7,	7,7,7,	7,7,7,	7,7,7	35.406	29.235
17.8125	7,	7,7,7,	7,7,7,	7,7,7,	13,13,13	35.533	27.058
17.1875	7,	7,7,7,	7,7,7,	13,13,13,	13,13,13	35.746	26.445
16.25	7,	7,7,7,	7,7,7,	19,19,19,	19,19,19	36.104	24.255
15.9375	7,	7,7,7,	7,7,7,	31,31,31,	31,31,31	36.241	21.694

4.1.4 Experimental Results

Two standard images, Barbara (512×512) and Lena (512×512), are used to test our scheme against others. In this chapter, we focus on the comparison of our proposed MDLVQ against the optimized MDSQ [5] since they are analogous except the quantization and related optimization schemes, although some other MD coding schemes are also included for reference. To make a fair comparison, the same experimental setup for the MDSQ scheme in [5] was applied here, that is, 10/18 Daubechies wavelet with four levels was used for wavelet decomposition, and target bit rate per channel is in the range 0.25–1 bpp. In Table 4.3, we present some example results of our optimized encoding parameters obtained for the standard images Barbara at the bit rate 0.5 bpp per channel, where N_S from Table 4.3, we can see at the bit rate 0.5 bpp per channel, while the volume-size δ_S decreases and the index number increases, the central PSNR values increase but the side PSNR values decrease, or vice versa. This is analogous to the variation of central and side PSNR values in MDSQ [5] as changing step size in SQ and the number of diagonals in MDSQ index assignment.

Figures 4.6 and 4.7 show the central and side distortion performance of the proposed MDLVQ scheme against the optimized MDSQ [5] for the two tested images at the bit rates of 0.25, 0.5, and 1 bpp per channel. Other two MD coders presented in [2] and [3] are also included for comparison. From the figures, we can clearly see that our proposed MDLVQ outperforms the tested MD image coders [2, 3]. Compared with the optimized MDSQ in [5], ours can still consistently improve around 0.2–0.4 dB for "Lena" and 0.5–0.7 dB for "Barbara" in central distortion with same or very close side distortions at the same bit rate. On the other hand, with similar central distortions, the proposed MDLVQ can achieve more improvement in side distortion compared with MDSQ [5], for example, about 2–5 dB for "Lena" and 3–5 dB for "Barbara" in side distortion for some points in Figs. 4.6 and 4.7.

It can be seen from Fig. 4.6 that the two algorithms reported in [6] and [10] have shown better performance than our proposed MDLVQ scheme. The possible reasons may lie in a few aspects, among which a typical and crucial reason is that different single-description image coders and entropy coders are employed in the two MD coders. It is known that the JPEG-2000 standard is developed to achieve excellent rate-distortion performance for single-description image coding, especially at low

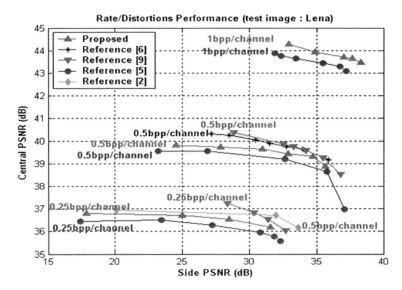

Fig. 4.6 Central and side PSNR results by the proposed coder and other referenced coders for "Lena"

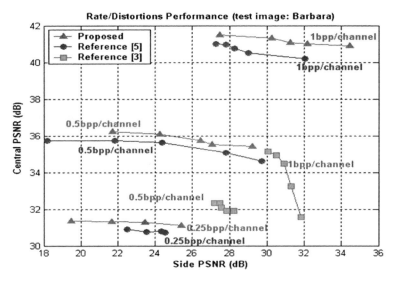

Fig. 4.7 Central and side PSNR results by the proposed coder and two referenced coders for "Barbara"

bit rate. It is reasonably conjectured that the gain of the MD image coders in [10] based on JPEG-2000 may come largely from better performance in the coding of each individual description using JPEG-2000. On the other hand, the Tarp filter image coder with classification for embedding (TCE) coder [9] has also exhibited very good rate-distortion performance in single-description image coding, which is comparable to JPEG-2000. The MD image coder in [6] is developed based on a modified MDSQ (MMDSQ) together with the TCE entropy coder, denoted as MMDSQ-TCE. It is explicitly stated in [6] that the efficiency of MMDSQ-TCE is partially due to the efficiency of the TCE coder, while the modified MDSQ adapts the efficient image coder naturally to an MD system.

To have a closer look at the different performance between the proposed MDLVQ scheme and the optimized MDSQ, Table 4.3 tabulates some representative pairs of central and side distortion results with respect to various bit rates for the image "Barbara." These representative pairs are points with good balance between central and side distortions in both schemes. From the results, we can find that our proposed MDLVQ consistently outperforms the optimized MDSQ [5] in both central and side distortion simultaneously at the same bit rate over a wide range from 0.25 to 1 bpp per channel, with both improvements of 0.688–2.436 dB in side distortion and 0.211–0.689 dB in central distortion.

4.1.5 Summary

An MD image coding scheme using MDLVQ has been developed in the section. Effective optimization schemes in both MDLVQ encoding and decoding have been accommodated in the proposed system to achieve better rate and central/side distortions performance. From the appropriate vector construction to the optimization of encoding parameters and optimized side decoding, the proposed MDLVQ has demonstrated superior rate-distortion performance to some other tested MD image coders including the optimized MDSQ image coder in [5]. Furthermore, in view of the fast LVQ encoding and similar computational complexity to the optimized MDSQ image coder in [5], our MDLVQ scheme is a worthy choice for MD coding [14].

4.2 Shifted LVQ-Based MDC

4.2.1 Motivation

In [4], Servetto, Vaishampayan, and Sloane developed a lattice-based multiple-description vector quantizer for balanced (symmetric) channels known as SVS technique, in which is claimed that the performance of MD hexagonal quantizer is consistently better than that of the MD scalar quantizer. The SVS technique can be reduced to the problem of mapping a fine lattice point to a label which consists of a pair of sub-lattice points, where the emphasis is to design the mapping function α

(also known as labeling function or equivalently index assignment) for minimizing side distortion $D_i (i = 1, 2)$ for a given fine lattice and sub-lattice. Central distortion D_0 is determined by the lattice vector quantization from an input vector to its closest fine lattice point. Side distortion, however, depends on the coarse degree of the sub-lattice, that is, the index N. In SVS technique, N is 7, 13, 19, 31, ..., which cannot make the sub-lattice points closest to the corresponding fine lattice points. Mentioned in [15], the side distortion increases monotonically with N, while the central distortion is not changed, so the gap between central and side distortions grows quickly as the index is increased. For a uniform source, at index $N = 13$, the central and side distortions differ by 16.8 dB [15]. The large gap for large index N is because as N increases, more sub-lattice points far away from the fine lattice have to be used to construct enough labels. Too large side distortion leads to an unacceptable side reconstruction, which is a deviation from the original intention of MD coding. So it is desirable to reduce the gap between the central and side distortions.

To address this problem, we present an MD technique based on shifted lattice vector quantization to effectively improve the side distortion and alleviate the gap between the central and side distortion [16]. Furthermore, the proposed technique reduces the encoding and decoding complexity compared with the SVS technique. In addition, although the lattice A_2 is used here to construct the MD quantizer, it is simple to extend other two-dimensional lattice such as Z_2 and D_2.

In [17], a scheme is proposed based on multiple-description uniform scalar quantization (MDUSQ) for robust and progressive transmission of images over unreliable channels, which outperforms the embedded MDC algorithm based on the polyphase transform proposed in [18]. However, another type of embedded scalar quantizers for MDC systems (EMDSQ) in [19] is claimed that provides constantly better rate-distortion performances on the central channel for all the rates.

In this chapter, a novel MD image coder is designed for progressive transmission over unreliable channels. There are mainly two significant improvements in the proposed scheme. On the one hand, according to the geometrical structure and the special relationship of lattice vector quantizers (LVQ), an MD quantizer called shifted lattice vector quantization (SLVQ) is constructed to produce two balanced descriptions as suggested in [20]. On the other hand, enlightened by EZW [11], in view of the characteristics of wavelet coefficients in different frequency sub-bands, a modified zerotree coding is applied for vectors of the lattice $A2$ in order to improve compression performance. It is noted that in our scheme, SLVQ is adopted instead of SVS-MDLVQ (developed by Servetto, Vaishampayan, and Sloane [4]) and [8] is also developed based on SVS-MDLVQ. The main reason is that in SVS-MDLVQ, only one LVQ on the central channel is difficult to match two zerotree coders on two channels, while in SLVQ, two LVQs respectively on both channels make it easy to cooperate with two zerotree coders for two descriptions (shown in Fig. 4.11).

Fig. 4.8 MDSLVQ for
unbalanced channels

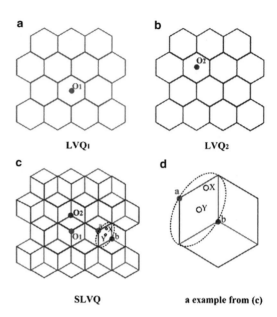

SLVQ   a example from (c)

4.2.2 MDSLVQ

Generally, lattice vector quantization is based on a certain geometrical structure of lattice, for example, the lattice A_2 is hexagonal lattice [12]. Here, we use the geometrical relationship between the same lattice vector quantizers to construct our MD quantizer for unbalanced channels and balanced channels. The latter has more practical applications, that is, the bit rate of two produced descriptions and the side distortions for the two side decoders are approximately the same.

4.2.2.1 MDSLVQ for Unbalanced Channels

Figure 4.8 illustrates the proposed MD technique MDSLVQ for two unbalanced channels.

SLVQ can be constructed by the two lattice vector quantizers called LVQ_1 and LVQ_2 for two channels in Fig. 4.8. The two lattice vector quantizers in Fig. 4.8, and b can be produced by the general method [12], but they have certain geometrical relationship in SLVQ, that is, LVQ_2 can be regarded as the shifted LVQ_1 when the origin O_1 is moved up to the origin O_2 and the shifted vector is $(0, 1/\sqrt{3})$. We can find that for LVQ_1 and LVQ_2, the hexagonal lattices can spread the whole space, while for SLVQ, the diamond lattices with different directions also can extend all the space. So the principle of MDSLVQ can be obtained as follows. The input source can be quantized coarsely by LVQ_1 and LVQ_2, respectively, to get two descriptions which can be transmitted on two channels. If only one channel works,

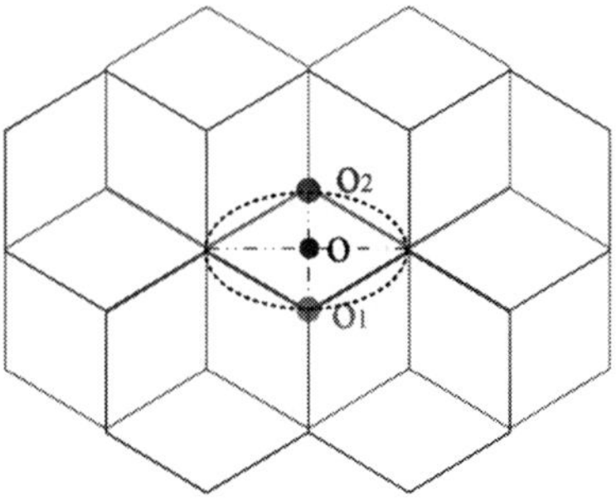

Fig. 4.9 MDSLVQ for two balanced channels

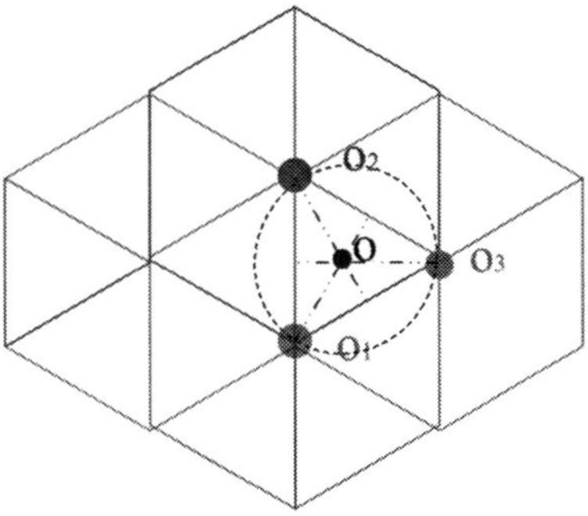

Fig. 4.10 MDSLVQ for three balanced channels

the reconstructive value is the lattice point in LVQ_1 or LVQ_2. If both channels work, the fine reconstruction is the centroid of the diamond lattice in SLVQ.

For example, an input two-dimensional vector X is quantized by LVQ_1 and LVQ_2 to get two lattice points, respectively, a and b. If only channel 1 or 2 works, the reconstructive value is just a or b. But if both channels work, the reconstruction is Y which is the centroid of diamond lattice (enclosed in ellipse illustrated in Fig. 4.8).

It is necessary to note that the origin O_1 of LVQ_1 is also used as the origin O of SLVQ, but the origin O_2 of LVQ_2 is not so. This will lead to the unbalance of LVQ_1 and LVQ_2 which will turn to the unbalance of two descriptions obtained. The reason behind is that the origins of LVQ_1 and LVQ_2 are not symmetrical according to the origin of SLVQ. As a result, the origin of SLVQ can be set on the centroid of the diamond lattice (enclosed in ellipse in Fig. 4.9) to realize the symmetry of O_1 and O_2 which turns to the balance of two descriptions.

4.2.2.2 MDSLVQ for Balanced Channels

As mentioned above, the reason behind the unbalanced descriptions obtained is that the origins of LVQ_1 and LVQ_2 are not symmetrical according to the origin of SLVQ. In Fig. 4.9, the origin of SLVQ is set on the centroid of the diamond lattice to realize the symmetry of O_1 and O_2.

In Fig. 4.10, by shifting the origin, three lattice vector quantizers can be used to construct three balanced descriptions. Here, we can also set the origin of SLVQ on

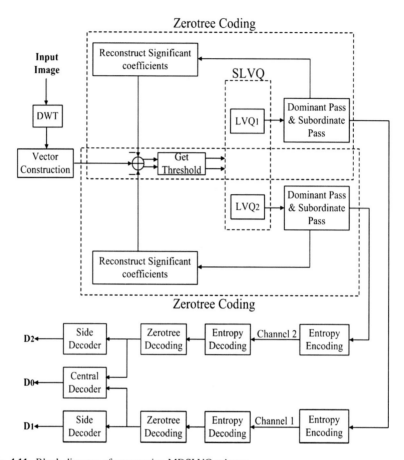

Fig. 4.11 Block diagram of progressive MDSLVQ scheme

the centroid of the triangle lattice shown in Fig. 4.10 to get symmetrical origins of lattice vector quantizers, which turns to produce three balanced descriptions. If only one channel works, the reconstruction is the lattice point of the hexagon lattice. If two arbitrary channels work, the reconstruction is the centroid of the diamond lattice just as in Fig. 4.8. Lastly, if all three channel work, the fine reconstruction is the centroid of the triangle lattice. As the descriptions achieved increase, we can obtain better reconstruction.

4.2.3   Progressive MDSLVQ Scheme

Our scheme can be depicted as in Fig. 4.11, and the encoding and decoding methods are explained as follows.

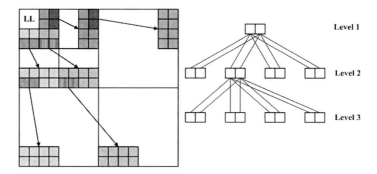

Fig. 4.12 The tree structure of wavelet coefficients

Fig. 4.13 The significant and insignificant wavelet coefficients

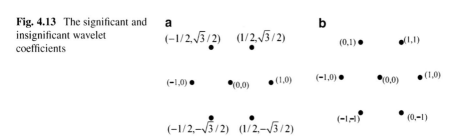

In MD encoding procedure, the image source is transformed by DWT, and then each frequency sub-band is scanned in different directions in view of corresponding directional correlation. Figure 4.2 shows our scheme for vector construction: HL is scanned to form vectors along vertical direction, LH is scanned in horizontal direction, and HH is scanned in zigzag way. In addition, spiral scan is also applied in LL sub-band considering the strong correlation among neighboring coefficients.

After vector construction, shifted lattice vector quantization and zerotree coding are applied to the reordered wavelet coefficients. Here, MDSLVQ for balanced channels can be adopted as in Sect. 4.2.2. Furthermore, modified zerotree coding is designed for the proposed scheme.

Figure 4.12 shows the tree structure of wavelet coefficients in different frequency sub-bands in the modified algorithm. Due to the lattice vector quantizer based on the lattice $A2$, two-dimensional vectors as tree nodes are considered in the modified zerotree coding. The zerotree here is also a quadtree of which all nodes are equal to or smaller than the root just like its concept in EZW [11]. Let us introduce the modified zerotree coding first.

The first step in the proposed zerotree coding is to get a threshold which is also the step size of lattice vector quantization [8]. In the modified algorithm, the step size can be computed to satisfy the case in which the significant wavelet coefficients have only six pairs $(1, 0)$, $(1, 1)$, $(0, 1)$, $(-1, 0)$, $(-1, -1)$, and $(0, -1)$ and the insignificant ones $(0, 0)$ as shown in Fig. 4.13. The idea to obtain such threshold comes from the fast algorithm of lattice vector quantization [21]. In [21], the lattice vector quantization based on the lattice $A2$ maps a two-dimensional vector to three-dimensional space first, then rounds off each dimensional value of three-dimensional vector to an integer, modifies the three-dimensional integer vector to make all three values from each dimension to add up to zero, and lastly maps again the three-dimensional vector to two-dimensional vector which is just the quantized vector. So if the maximum among three-dimensional values is chosen as the step size of lattice vector quantization, that is, the threshold in modified zerotree coding, the insignificant pair $(0, 0)$ and six significant ones can be achieved as in Fig. 4.13. Additionally, the lattice $A2$ can be spanned by the vectors $(1, 0)$ and $(-1/2, \sqrt{3}/2)$ [11], so if we use these two vectors as base vectors, we can utilize Fig. 4.13b instead of Fig. 4.13.

Just like the conventional algorithm EZW, the modified zerotree coding also has two passes. In the first pass, the dominant pass, the quantized wavelet image is scanned in different directions in view of corresponding directional correlation, as mentioned above, and then the symbols are produced for every two-dimensional vector. If the quantized pair is $(1, 0)$, $(1, 1)$, or $(0, 1)$, it will be regarded as positive significant coefficients, and a symbol "p" is outputted. If the quantized pair is $(-1, 0)$, $(-1, -1)$, or $(0, -1)$, it will be negative significant coefficients denoted by a symbol "n." If $(0, 0)$ is the quantized pair and all of its children nodes (shown in Fig. 4.12) are also $(0, 0)$, it is the root of zerotree and a symbol "t" is obtained. However, if the quantized pair is $(0, 0)$ and not all of its children nodes are $(0, 0)$, it is the isolated zero and denoted by "z." In second pass, the subordinate pass, only the significant quantized pairs which have been denoted by "p" or "n," three symbols "a," "b," and "c" are used as the division of $(1, 0)$, $(1, 1)$, and $(0, 1)$ in the case of positive pairs or of $(-1, 0)$, $(-1, -1)$, and $(0, -1)$ in the case of negative pairs.

After the two passes, the significant pairs denoted by "p" and "n" can be reconstructed to a two-dimensional vector which is subtracted from the original two-dimensional vector before lattice vector quantization. At the same time, the insignificant pairs denoted by "t" and "z" will be kept unchangeable, that is, $(0, 0)$. Then the next threshold will be computed by the reconstructed wavelet coefficients, and the zerotree coding is used in succession. As a result, a loop is formed (enclosed in the broken line in Fig. 4.11).

The above mentioned is the proposed zerotree coding, which may produce two descriptions. Then after entropy encoding, two descriptions are transmitted over two channels. It need be explained that the entropy encoding is used for the bit stream from two pass of zerotree coding, but the threshold which nearly can be neglected is coded by fixed length bits.

In decoding procedure, after entropy decoding, the bitstreams are processed by zerotree decoding. It is noted that for each loop or each threshold, the zerotree decoding is lossless. Consequently, if the two channels work, the fine reconstruction is just the centroid of the diamond lattice in SLVQ. If only one channel works, the lattice point of the hexagonal lattice can be regarded as coarse reconstruction.

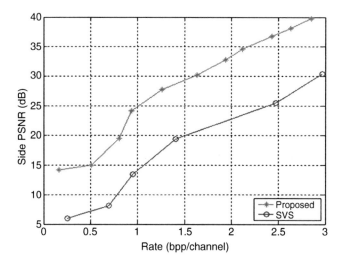

Fig. 4.14 Side PSNR values for the test image Lena (512 × 512)

4.2.4 Experimental Results

Next, we will introduce the performance of the proposed schemes. Firstly, MD-SLVQ is compared with SVS technique to show its improved characteristics. Then, we will discuss the performance of progressive MDSLVQ scheme compared with other progressive ones.

4.2.4.1 MDSLVQ Versus SVS Scheme

Here, we consider two balanced channels. To make a fair comparison, the standard image Lena (512 × 512) is coded and decoded directly by the proposed MDSLVQ and SVS technique [4], respectively. In a conventional two-dimensional rate-distortion perspective, Figs. 4.14 and 4.15 show the side and central rate-distortion performance of the proposed MDSLVQ against the SVS technique. From the figures, we can find that our proposed MDSLVQ consistently outperforms the SVS technique in both central and side distortion simultaneously at the same bit rate over a wide range from 0.25 to 3 bpp per channel, with about 9 dB improvement for side distortion in Fig. 4.4 and about 3 dB for central distortion in Fig. 4.5. In Fig. 4.14, the index N in SVS technique is 7 to obtain the best side distortion.

Figure 4.16 shows the gap between central and side distortion at the bit rate from 0.25 to 3 bpp per channel. It is observed from the figure that when the index is 7, the gap between central and side distortion is about 9–11 dB. However, the gap of the proposed technique can keep 4 dB approximately. As a result, the gap has been effectively reduced by the proposed technique.

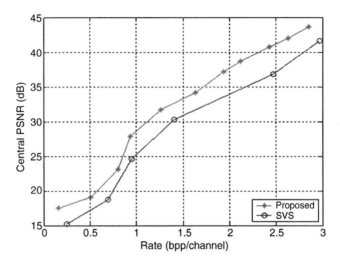

Fig. 4.15 Central PSNR values for the test image Lena (512×512)

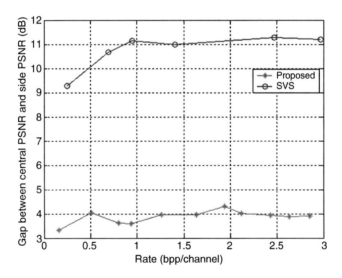

Fig. 4.16 The gap between central and side PSNR values for the test image Lena (512×512)

For a more general experiment, a uniform distributed random source is constructed at the interval [0, 255] with the size 512×512.

Figures 4.17 and 4.18 show the side and central rate-distortion performance of the proposed MDSLVQ compared with the SVS technique. And Fig. 4.19 illustrates the gap between central and side distortions further. From the figures, we can see the same results as the experiment for the standard image Lena. The proposed technique can achieve better performance than the SVS technique in both central and side distortion. Especially, the gap between central and side distortion has been reduced effectively by MDSLVQ.

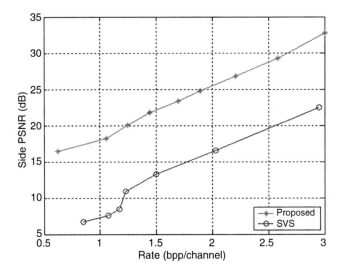

Fig. 4.17 Side PSNR values for the test uniform distributed random source

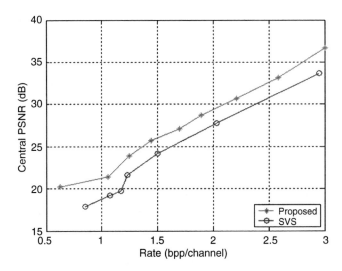

Fig. 4.18 Central PSNR values for the test uniform distributed random source

4.2.4.2   Progressive MDSLVQ Versus Other Schemes

Here, the standard image Lena (512×512) is also chosen to validate the performance of the proposed scheme MDSLVQ. Figures 4.20 and 4.21 show the side and
central distortion-rate performance of the proposed scheme against EMDSQ [19]
and MDUSQ [17], respectively.

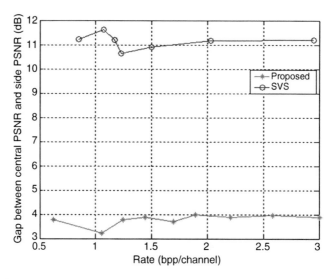

Fig. 4.19 The gap between central and side PSNR for the test uniform distributed random source

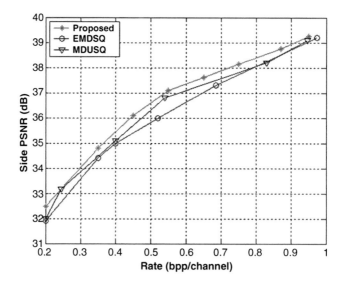

Fig. 4.20 PSNR results from only one channel

From the figures, we can find that our proposed MDSLVQ consistently outperforms the other schemes in both central and side distortion simultaneously at the progressive bit rate over a wide range from 0.2 to 1 bpp per channel, with about 0.2–0.5 dB improvement for side PSNR values in Fig. 4.20 and about 1–1.5 dB for central PSNR values in Fig. 4.21.

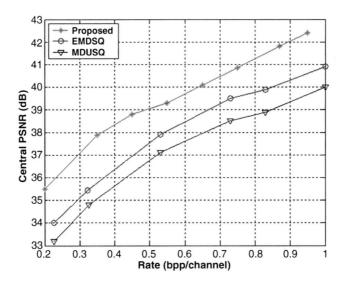

Fig. 4.21 PSNR results from both channels

4.2.5 Summary

Firstly, an MD technique using shifted lattice vector quantization (MDSLVQ) has been presented in the chapter to achieve a better trade-off among rate and central/side distortion. The shifted lattice vector quantizer takes full advantage of geometrical structure and spatial relationship of hexagonal lattice to construct balanced or unbalanced MD descriptions. From the experimental results, the proposed MDSLVQ has demonstrated superior rate-distortion performance to the popular MD lattice vector quantization SVS technique [4].

Then, a novel MD scheme for progressive wavelet image coding has been presented based on shifted lattice vector quantization. The SLVQ takes advantages of geometrical structure and keeps better redundancy between quantized wavelet coefficients to construct progressive MD descriptions. The modified zerotree coding reorders the wavelet coefficients efficiently to improve the compression performance. From the experimental results, the proposed scheme has demonstrated better rate-distortion performance to the other MD schemes [19] and [17] for progressive wavelet image coding.

4.3 Diversity-Based MDC

4.3.1 Motivation

In the above sections, we introduced some MD algorithms for image. For example, multiple-description scalar quantization (MDSQ) is one of the first practical MDC schemes, which is applied to wavelet-based image coding in [5]. A modified MDSQ (MMDSQ) is designed and applied to image coding in [6]. Pair-wise correlation transform is presented in [22], and multiple-description lattice vector quantization (MDLVQ) based image coding is developed in [14]. All of the above methods exploit some single-description (SD) image coders with MDC adaptations to strike a central-side coding trade-off.

In [23], a novel MD scheme based on diversity is employed for speech coding, and the transform diversity is applied to image coding in [24]. For the diversity-based MDC approaches, some existing single-description image coding schemes are adopted with little change, which facilitates the easy implementation. More importantly, the central coding performance can still be improved even when the side coder achieves the same best performance as its corresponding single-description coder at a rate. However, it becomes difficult to achieve a flexible central-side coding trade-off with the diversity-based MDC scheme, which may limit its applications. We present a two-stage diversity-based MDC scheme, in which the trade-offs between central and side coding performance can be tuned easily and flexibly [25]. More importantly, in the side decoder, we find that the side reconstruction quality can be improved by taking into account the subsampled central decoded errors appended to each description in the second stage. Note that in the two-stage MMDSQ [6], the second stage information can only reduce the central distortion but to no avail for side distortion when only one description is received. In contrast, our proposed two-stage diversity-based MDC scheme can help improve not only the central coding performance but also the side performance with the second stage information. Moreover, the proposed scheme can be generalized to description coding easily.

4.3.2 Overview

In the context of MDC, diversities may be presented as path diversity, time diversity, spatial diversity, and coder diversity [23]. MDC itself can be seen as a path diversity scheme where multiple descriptions can be delivered through different paths. Coding signal and its delayed version or the version of its elementary transformation can form the time or spatial diversity, while adopting different coding schemes for descriptions can lead to coder diversity. In the proposed balanced MDC scheme, the spatial diversity is employed, that is, the diversity is obtained by image shifting/rotating.

4.3.2.1 Diversity-Based Two-Description Image Coding

A diversity-based two-description image coding scheme is shown in Fig. 4.1. An image is wavelet-transformed (WT) and is coded by the QTCQ approach [26] to produce description 1. To generate description 2, the image is rotated by 180° and

Fig. 4.22 Diversity-based
two-description coding with
QTCQ

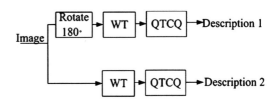

then goes through the same coding process as for the first description. When both descriptions are received, they are decoded and averaged to get a better central reconstruction. Since the wavelet coefficients of the original image and that of the rotated image are different, this diversity can also be considered as transform diversity.

QTCQ has shown its superior performance in image coding [26], which uses the quadtree structure to classify wavelet coefficients and applies TCQ to quantize the classified wavelet coefficients. It is known that quantizing the signal and its elementary transformation version with vector quantizer (VQ) can form diversity [23]. Therefore, using QTCQ can help to further enhance the diversity because the quantization style of TCQ is similar to that of VQ.

4.3.2.2 Distortion Analysis

For the coding scheme in Fig. 4.22, assume $\hat{x}_1$ and $\hat{x}_2$ are the side reconstructed counterparts of an original wavelet coefficient x, respectively, as

$$\hat{x}_1 = x + e_1 \tag{4.5}$$

$$\hat{x}_2 = x + e_2, \tag{4.6}$$

where e_1 and e_2 denote the errors generated in the side encoding. The central reconstruction is just the average of the two side ones

$$\hat{x}_0 = 0.5\,(\hat{x}_1 + \hat{x}_2) = x + 0.5(e_1 + e_2). \tag{4.7}$$

In view of the same coding mechanism for the two balanced descriptions, we assume the errors have the same mean of zero and same variance of δ^2. Then, the side distortion d_1 and d_2 are almost the same; therefore, only d_1 is given, as follows:

$$d_1 = E\left[(x - \hat{x}_1)^2\right] = E\left[e_1^2\right] = \delta^2. \tag{4.8}$$

The central distortion d_0 is

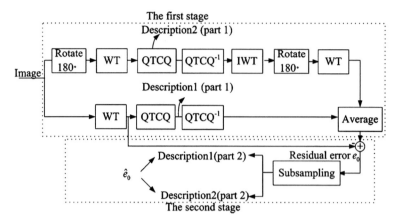

Fig. 4.23 Proposed two-stage diversity-based MD image coding scheme

$$
\begin{aligned}
d_0 &= E\left[(x - \hat{x}_1)^2\right] = E\left[0.5(e_1 + e_2)^2\right] \\
&= E\left[0.25\left(e_1^2 + e_2^2\right)\right] + 0.5E\left[e_1 e_2\right] \\
&= 0.5\delta^2(1 + \rho) \le \delta^2,
\end{aligned}
\tag{4.9}
$$

where ρ is the correlation coefficient between e_1 and e_2. It shows that the central distortion will be lower than the side distortion if ρ is less than 1. If the error e_i of each description is uncorrelated to each other, that is, $\rho = 0$, the central distortion will only be half of the side distortion. This can be translated to a 3 dB gain in the central distortion over the side distortion. A larger gain can be achieved if the errors of the two descriptions are negatively correlated. We can see that the gap between the central distortion and side distortion depends on the correlation coefficient ρ that is in turn determined by the selected diversity scheme. It is at least not straightforward if not hard as well as not easily manageable by designing different diversity schemes to change ρ, which makes the tuning of central-side distortion trade-off very troublesome and difficult. Therefore, we consider adopting a second stage based on the scheme in Fig. 4.1 for an easy and flexible control of the trade-off.

4.3.3 Two-Stage Diversity-Based Scheme

4.3.3.1 Proposed Two-Description Coding Scheme

The proposed two-stage diversity-based two-description coding scheme is illustrated in Fig. 4.23. Each description comprises two parts formed in the first and the second stage, respectively. Part 1 is generated as that in Fig. 4.22, and then the residuals are obtained by subtracting the central (averaged) reconstruction in stage 1 from the original wavelet coefficients. The wavelet residuals are split by subsampling and coded with QTCQ to produce part 2 information for each description.

Note that the MMDSQ [6] also uses a similar two-stage structure. When both descriptions are received, the second stage decoded information (part 2) is added to the average of the description 1 (part 1) and description two (part 1) to further enhance the reconstruction quality, which is similar to the MMDSQ central decoding [6]. However, the side decoding of the proposed scheme is much different from that of MMDSQ. In the side decoding of the proposed scheme, when only one description is received, the reconstructed information from part 2 will also be exploited to be added to the part 1 of the received description, which will be shown to help reduce the side distortion in the following. In the MMDSQ [6], however, when only one description is received, the second part information is completely useless, which cannot be used for improving the side decoding and therefore discarded.

4.3.3.2   Side Distortion Analysis

The residual errors between the original wavelet coefficients and the averaged reconstructions from part 1 information can be represented as

$$e_0 = x - \hat{x}_0 = -0.5(e_1 + e_2). \tag{4.10}$$

The errors are split with subsampling and then coded by QTCQ to form the second part for each description. For simplicity, we assume the odd/even coefficient subsampling way. For the balanced descriptions, only description 1 is considered, while the other can be analyzed similarly. In the decoding end, the odd samples of the second part are added to the first part of description 1. Then, description 1 becomes

$$\hat{x}_1' = \begin{cases} x + e_1 + \hat{e}_0, & \text{for odd coeficients} \\ x + e_1, & \text{for even coeficients} \end{cases}, \tag{4.11}$$

where $\hat{e}_0$ denotes the reconstructed counterpart of e_0. We make the asymptotic analysis of adding the decoded odd part of central residuals to the side reconstruction, that is, $\hat{e}_0$ approximates e_0. Substituting e_0 with that in (4.10), we can obtain the side distortion for description 1 as

$$d_1' = E\left[(x - \hat{x}_1')^2\right] = 0.5E\left[(e_1)^2\right] + 0.5E\left[(e_1 + e_0)^2\right]$$

$$= 0.5\delta^2 + 0.25\delta^2(1 - \rho) \leq \delta^2. \tag{4.12}$$

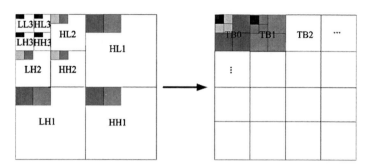

Fig. 4.24 Subsampling method

The side distortion for description 2 can also be obtained as (4.12) in the balanced coding. The equality of the above formula is valid only when $\rho = -1$, which means no reduction of side distortion. In this case, however, the central distortion will be zero which can be seen from (4.9), thus no residual error and no bit cost in the second stage. For $0 \le \rho < 1$ which is observed in our experiments, the second stage information can help reduce the side distortion from δ^2 to the range of $0.5\delta^2 \sim 0.75\delta^2$.

In view of the strong correlation in wavelet subbands, we consider subsampling the coefficients in a way of odd/even wavelet tree block to facilitate the following QTCQ for a better compression. Taking a three-level wavelet transform as an example, the subsampling approach is shown in Fig. 4.24, which is like the zerotree structure. That is, the wavelet coefficients in different sub-bands corresponding to the same spatial location are grouped to form a tree block, and then these blocks are subsampled in an odd/even way.

4.3.3.3   Flexible Trade-Off Control

In the proposed two-stage scheme, the trade-off between the central and side distortion is tuned by the bit rate allocation in the first and the second stage. When the channel condition is bad, less or no bits will be allocated to the second stage, to favor side decoding. In the case of skipping the second stage, the side coding performance may be maximized, which is equivalent to a corresponding SD scheme at the same side coding rate, and the central performance can still be enhanced to some extent due to the diversity. Note that in the same case of skipping the second stage in MMDSQ (degraded to normal MDSQ), if the side coding performance is maximized, the central performance will be the same as that without any further improvement. When the network condition is good, more or even all the bits are assigned to the second part to favor central decoding. When allocating all the bits to the second stage, each of the bit streams contains half of the information, and the central coding performance will be improved significantly. In between for the bit allocation, varying central-side coding trade-offs can be obtained.

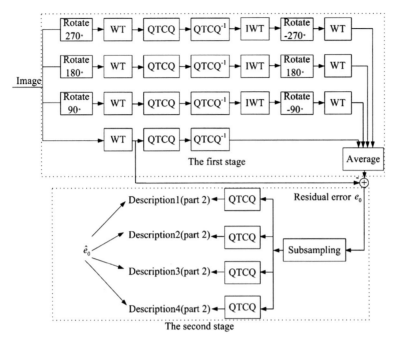

Fig. 4.25 Proposed four-description image coding

4.3.3.4   Extension to Four-Description Coding

The proposed scheme can be generalized to description scheme conveniently. As an example, 4-description coding is illustrated in Fig. 4.25. The residual error is subsampled in the similar tree block way. In the decoding end, if two or more descriptions are received, the first parts are decoded and averaged before adding the second decoded parts.

4.3.4   Experimental Results

4.3.4.1   The Two-Description Coding

For the sake of comparison, we also give the performance of MDSQ-based wavelet coder by Servetto et al. [5], modified MDSQ based on Tarp filter image coder with classification for embedding (MMDSQ+TCE) [6], the transform and data fusion scheme [24], the JPEG2000-based MD approach [10], and feature-oriented MDC (FOMDC) [27]. All of the five methods including ours make use of wavelet transform in their coding scheme. A six-level wavelet decomposition is applied with the Daubechies 9/7 filters, and 8-state TCQ is used in the QTCQ scheme. The

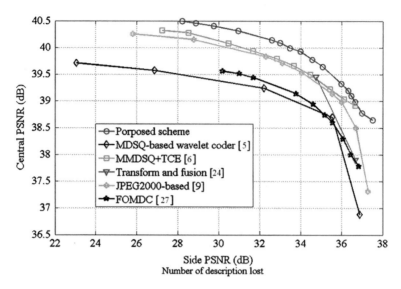

Fig. 4.26 Comparison of central-side PSNR curves at 0.5 bpp/description for "Lena"

tested rate is selected to be 0.5 bpp per description. The central and side PSNR performance for "Lena" (of size 512×512) is shown in Fig. 4.26. Due to the page limit, the result on another image "Barbara" is not included which exhibits the similar performance.

It can be seen from the figure that the proposed scheme achieves the best central-side distortion performance at the rate of 0.5 bpp per description. Note that the transform and data fusion scheme [7] has only the first stage structure of the proposed scheme, thus, as mentioned before, making it difficult to achieve varying trade-off points, where only two trade-off points are obtained. With our two-stage scheme, the trade-off points can be obtained conveniently and flexibly by changing the bit allocation in the two stages, where many points are indicated in the figure. Furthermore, we can see that as side PSNR increases with more redundancy introduced, the central PSNR will drop dramatically to be close to the side PSNR for the schemes like in [5, 10], and [27], whereas in our proposed scheme with few bits for the second stage, the central PSNR is still better than the side PSNR over 1–2 dB. The better central-side coding performance is due to the high-performance QTCQ coding as well as our proposed two-stage MDC scheme. For example, in the single-description coding for "Lena," the QTCQ coder can obtain 40.75 dB of PSNR at 1 bpp which outperforms JPEG-2000 around 0.3 dB, while our proposed MDC scheme can achieve about 1 dB gain in average over the JPEG-2000-based MDC in side distortion performance given a central distortion at the total rate of 1 bpp, as can be seen in Fig. 4.5. The complexity for the proposed scheme increases since two stages are involved. Running on a 2.99-GHz Pentium computer with Windows XP Professional, it takes around 2.23 s to encode a 512×512 image into two descriptions at 0.5 bpp/description, and 1.81 s to decode two side descriptions

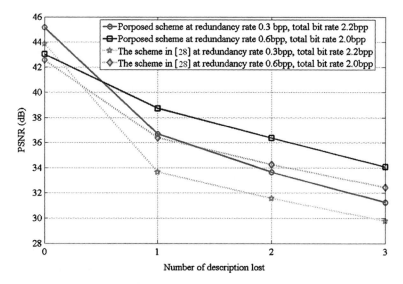

Fig. 4.27   Comparison of four-description coding for "Lena"

and one central description, without any program optimization. The JPEG-2000-based MDC scheme, however, requires longer running time on the same platform, that is, about 6 s for encoding and 3 s for decoding.

4.3.4.2   The Four-Description Coding

The four-description coding results are shown in Fig. 4.27 to compare the proposed scheme against the JPEG2000-based MD scheme [28] for the image "Lena" at the total target rate of 2.2 and 2.0 bpp with two redundancy rates of 0.3 and 0.6 bpp, respectively. For the JPEG2000-based scheme, we use the software available in the website [28], which, to our observation, cannot always assure an accurate total bit rate for a given redundancy rate. By adjusting the quantization in the two stages, our two-stage coder is easy to tune to produce the same total bit rate and redundancy rate as that of the JPEG2000-based scheme. In our scheme, the rate of the first stage is considered as the redundancy rate. It can be seen that the proposed scheme consistently and significantly outperforms the JPEG2000-based scheme at the two redundancy rates in the case of losing one or more descriptions.

4.3.5   Summary

A two-stage diversity-based MD scheme has been proposed for a flexible central/side distortion trade-off. More importantly, the second stage information for each description obtained by subsampling the central residual errors from the first stage has been shown to improve the side coding performance in addition to the central performance. The scheme can be extended to n-description coding in a convenient way. The experiment results on image coding have shown the superior central/side coding performance of the proposed scheme over a few state-of-the-art MD approaches.

4.4   Steganography-Based MDC

4.4.1   Motivation

Lots of MD coding techniques have been developed using different strategies for coding various data like speech, audio, image, and video. One of the most classical methods is multiple-description scalar quantization (MDSQ) [29], which was successfully applied in image coding [5]. The pair-wise correlating transform (PCT) was exploited in [22]. MD lattice vector quantization (MDLVQ) has also shown promising results for image coding [14]. Another popular two-description scheme partitions an (transformed) image into two parts, for example, part 1 and part 2, each of which goes through a fine coding as well as a coarse coding. Then one description is formed by concatenating the finely coded part 1 and the coarsely coded part 2, while the other description is complementarily generated by combining the coarsely coded part 1 with the finely coded part 2. Such MD coding schemes can be found in [27, 30, 31].

In this section, we propose a novel two-description image coding scheme. As usual, each description of an image is constructed by a finely coded part (fine information) and another coarsely coded part (coarse information) [32]. The new scheme features that the coarse information is embedded (hidden) into the fine information selectively using, such as an LSB steganographic method [33]. In this way, coarse information can be carried on the fine information freely without allocating any more bit budget for the coarse information. A method combining MD coding and data hiding scheme was proposed in [34], where the DC value is replicated and embedded into the available AC coefficients in both descriptions for DCT-based two-description coding. Compared with that simple method, our scheme is different in the MD coding design and embedding approach. More details for our design will be elaborated in the following sections.

4.4.2   Basic Idea and Related Techniques

Consider partitioning an image into two parts in the block checkerboard manner, where the partition can be done in the spatial or wavelet domain. A block partition

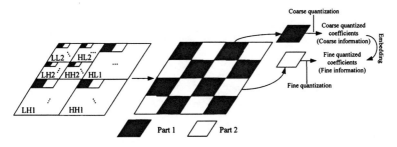

Fig. 4.28 Basic idea of the two-description image coding with steganography

in the spatial domain is simple, while the block partition in the wavelet domain normally produces better coding performance, where the wavelet coefficients in different sub-bands corresponding to the same spatial location are grouped to form tree-structured blocks. Figure 4.28 shows such a block checkerboard partition in the wavelet domain.

4.4.2.1   Fine and Coarse Coding

Two sub-images are grouped by part 1 and part 2 blocks in Fig. 4.28, respectively. The wavelet coefficients of part 1 sub-image are quantized by a coarse quantizer, and the quantized coefficients are referred to be coarse information. The wavelet coefficients of part 2 are quantized by a fine quantizer to produce fine information. The coarse information is embedded (hidden) into the fine information. Note that the length of the coarse information (denoted as L) needs to be transmitted for extracting purpose, and the bit cost for the length is trivial and negligible. For example, for a 512×512 image with 0.1 bpp coarse information, the bit cost for the length representation is about $\log_2 (0.1 \times 512^2) \doteq 15$ bits, which amounts to an overhead of $15/(512 \times 512) = 5.9 \times 10^{-5}$ bit-per-pixel (bpp).

4.4.2.2   Embedding Approach – LSB Steganographic Method

Steganography can send message under the cover of a carrier signal, and many techniques of steganography have been proposed [33, 35]. One of the well-known steganographic methods is the LSB substitution which replaces the least-significant bits of coefficients with the information bits. In this section, the LSB steganographic method is exploited to embed the coarse information in the least-significant bits of the fine information selectively. The process of the LSB steganographic method is shown in Fig. 4.29.

The principle of the LSB steganographic method is to change the LSB of nonzero quantized wavelet coefficients to match the coarse information bit stream in the following way:

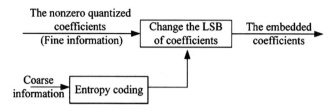

Fig. 4.29 LSB steganographic method

$$e\_w_i = \begin{cases} \tilde{w}_i, & \text{if mod } (\tilde{w}_i, 2) = c_j \\ \tilde{w}_i + 1, & \text{if mod } (\tilde{w}_i, 2) \neq c_j \, \& \, \text{mod } (\tilde{w}_i, 2) = 1 \\ \tilde{w}_i - 1, & \text{if mod } (\tilde{w}_i, 2) \neq c_j \, \& \, \text{mod } (\tilde{w}_i, 2) = 0 \end{cases} \qquad (4.13)$$

where e_w_i is the embedded wavelet coefficient, $\tilde{w}_i$ is the original nonzero quantized wavelet coefficient, mod (,) is the module operation, and c_j, $j = 1, \ldots, L$ is the jth bit in the coarse information bit stream.

The information extracting is simple, which can be obtained by

$$c_j = \text{mod}(e\_w_i, 2). \qquad (4.14)$$

4.4.3 Proposed Two-Description Image Coding Scheme

The proposed two-description image coding scheme based on wavelet domain partition is sketched in Fig. 4.30, including encoding and decoding processes. A similar coding structure can be obtained if spatial partitioning is considered.

4.4.3.1 Information Embedding

The coarse coefficients (coarse information) are embedded into the nonzero quantized wavelet coefficients selected from high frequency to the low frequency for minimizing the degradation of the fine coefficients with the LSB steganographic method introduced in Sect. 4.4.2.2, if L is smaller than the number of the nonzero quantized wavelet coefficients. There are two points which need to be considered in the embedding process.

1. *Embedding Capacity*: The embedding capacity depends on the number of nonzero quantized wavelet coefficients. When the coarse information amount is larger than the embedded capacity, a combination of embedding and appending the coarse information can be employed. That means some coarse information is embedded in the fine information, while the rest will be appended after the fine information.

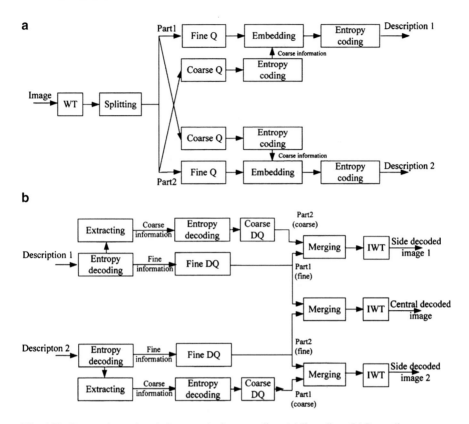

Fig. 4.30 Proposed two-description wavelet image coding. (**a**) Encoding. (**b**) De-coding

2. *Embedding Performance*: The embedding of coarse information suggests that the coarse information can be delivered freely (with zero bit rate), which can enhance the side decoding performance when only one description is correctly received. On the other hand, the embedding will affect the quality of the fine information decoding, which may compromise the central decoding performance for two descriptions received correctly. Note that the LSB embedding method expressed in (4.13) may not necessarily change the fine information, in view that the LSB of the coefficient $\tilde{w}_i$ only changes when $\mathrm{mod}(\tilde{w}_i, 2) \neq c_j$, which accounts for around 50% possibility. In this sense, the "free" coarse information can be obtained with the embedding scheme at the cost of a possible degradation of fine information. We would point out that the fine information degradation is normally low, in that only the LSB is changed, and the wavelet coefficients are selected from high frequency to low frequency. It is rational to infer that the best way can be to calculate the coding gain and loss, respectively, and then to decide whether or not such an embedding of some bits in some selected coefficients should proceed. Reversible data hiding may also be considered for optimization.

We would like to highlight that the embedding of coarse information into the fine information is very different from simply lending one bit from fine information representation to the coarse information representation (that is again the concatenating of fine and coarse information). In our embedding scheme, the encoded coarse information is embedded into finely quantized wavelet coefficients selectively, and then the coefficients are entropy coded. In this way, coarse information is included, while the finely quantized wavelet coefficients are encoded with only a slight degradation, as to be shown in our following experiments. Also as pointed out above, the embedding may not necessarily change the LSB of the finely quantized wavelet coefficients, and thus, some pieces of fine information may not be affected at all while the coarse information is embedded.

Here, we consider embedding all the coarse information into the fine information to check the feasibility and effectiveness of the proposed approach. Further extension and optimization mentioned above will be done in the next step.

4.4.3.2 Discriminative Quantization

Considering that the LSB of the nonzero quantized wavelet coefficients may be changed for information embedding which may lead to an appreciable change if the quantization step is large, a discriminative quantization scheme is exploited which employs a finer quantization for the nonzero quantized coefficients selected for embedding. Firstly, all the wavelet coefficients are quantized by a uniform quantizer with a quantization step size of q_1. Then for those nonzero quantized coefficients chosen for embedding, a smaller quantization step size (q_2) is discriminatively applied for the finer quantization of the coefficients sequentially from the highest frequency to the lowest frequency. The number of the finely quantized coefficients depends on the amount of the coarse information to be embedded, which is indicated by the coarse encoder described in Sect. 4.4.2.

4.4.3.3 Decoding

When both descriptions are received, the finely coded information from each description is used for the reconstruction of the central decoded image. When only one description is available, the coarse information can be extracted from the received description, which is then decoded to complement the decoded fine information for a side decoded image.

4.4.4 Experimental Results

Six standard images (512×512) are used as the testing images, and the 10–18 Daubechies wavelet is employed. For the coarse information, the quantization value is chosen from 65 to 210 for different bit rates tested, where all the coarse information can be embedded into the fine information. By adjusting the finer quantization value q_1 from 8 to 65, the bit rate per description varies, and q_2 is selected as 2 for a small modification due to embedding.

For a fair comparison, we tested our proposed embedding-based coding scheme against the following two conventional methods without such embedding, with the same coarse and fine coders for the two parts. That is to say, the fine information and the coarse information used for the three testing schemes are exactly the same.

1. *Coarse Information Skipping*: In the coarse information skipping approach, each description only contains the fine information from the fine coder and skips the coarse information, resulting in the same coding rate per description as in our coarse information embedding scheme. In this way, the redundancy between the two descriptions is minimized to favor the central decoding performance. When only one description is received, an interpolation method used in [36] is exploited to recover the missing part.
2. *Coarse Information Appending*: In the coarse information appending scheme, the coarse information is appended after the fine information. Each description is produced by concatenating the fine information and the coarse information for the two parts alternatively. Note that the coarse information and the fine information used in this scheme are the same as those in the proposed scheme.

Figures 4.31 and 4.32 plot the rate-distortion performance of side/central coding to compare our proposed method against the other two relevant schemes on two testing images, respectively. Both spatial and wavelet domain partitions are considered in the comparison, where 8×8 blocks are used for the spatial splitting, and 32×32 tree-structured blocks are for the wavelet domain splitting. In the experiment, the bit rate of coarse information ranges from 0.05 to 0.12 bpp. As mentioned before, in this letter, we consider all the coarse information to be embedded into the fine information. We take the spatial domain partition as an example for the following discussions. It can be seen from Figs. 4.31a and 4.32a that, for the side coding, the proposed method outperforms the coarse information skipping approach substantially as the bit rate increases, for example, over 3 dB gain for "Lena" and 4 dB gain for "Barbara." Compared with the coarse information appending method, the proposed scheme can achieve the similar decoded quality (PSNR) with a lower bit rate up to 12.9% rate reduction for "Lena" and 12.6% rate reduction for "Barbara." For the central coding, the coarse information skipping method achieves the best central decoded results as expected, at the expense of the poorest side decoded results described above. Figures 4.31b and 4.32b demonstrate that the proposed one achieves similar results (with a PSNR degradation less than 0.6% and 0.8% for "Lena" and "Barbara," respectively) as the coarse information skipping method in central coding, and significantly better results than the coarse information appending scheme due to the bit rate saving. From the results, we can clearly see that our proposed scheme achieves overall better coding results than the two conventional methods in terms of side and central distortion-rate performance.

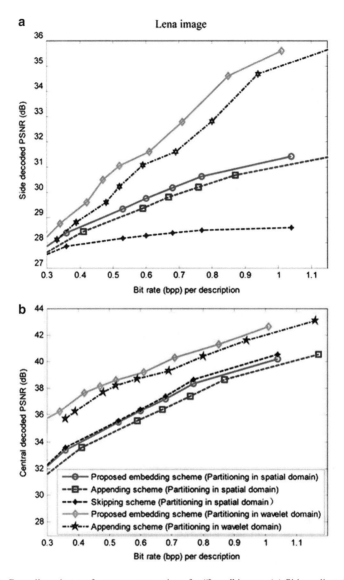

Fig. 4.31 Rate-distortion performance comparison for "Lena" image. (**a**) Side coding. (**b**) Central coding

If we compare the results based on the wavelet domain partition, the figures also clearly demonstrate that the proposed scheme significantly outperforms the appending method, where the improvement is more noticeable, especially for side decoded results, than that based on the spatial partition. The skipping scheme produces very poor side coding results due to the difficulty of interpolating the missing part based on the wavelet domain partition, which is far from the proposed and appending schemes and therefore not shown in the figures. As expected,

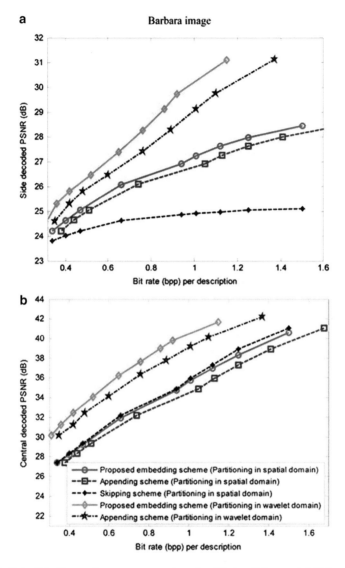

Fig. 4.32 Rate-distortion performance comparison for "Barbara" image. (**a**) Side coding. (**b**) Central coding

the wavelet domain partition can achieve better coding performance than the spatial partition. In short, our proposed embedding scheme exhibits superior coding efficiency to the other two conventional approaches in either partition case.

To save space due to the page limit, we cannot include more rate-distortion curves but instead tabulate the results for the other four testing images in Table 4.5 based on spatial domain partition for comparison, which further show the coding gains

Table 4.5 Comparison of side/central coding results for the three tested schemes

Image	Rate (bpp)	Proposed Side/central PSNR (dB)	Skipping Side/central PSNR (dB)	Appending Rate (bpp)	Side/central PSNR (dB)
Pepper	0.64	28.70/34.40	28.26/34.49	0.71	28.70/34.49
Elain	0.62	29.45/32.85	29.11/32.88	0.68	29.45/32.88
Goldhill	0.76	28.70/33.06	27.96/33.09	0.85	28.70/33.09
Girl	0.62	30.43/36.99	29.44/37.16	0.68	30.44/37.16

of the proposed scheme over the other two conventional methods. The following parameter settings were used in our experiment: $q_1 = 30$, $q_2 = 2$ for the results in the table.

4.4.5 Summary

In this section, a new idea for designing two-description coding with steganography has been presented. Instead of concatenating the two encoded parts to construct a description, one coarsely coded part is embedded into the other finely coded part using the LSB steganographic method. A specific embedding-based two-description image coding scheme has been developed and tested to demonstrate the effectiveness of the proposed scheme with very encouraging results.

4.5 Adaptive Temporal Sampling Based MDC

4.5.1 Motivation

In the past years, the MDC of still image has attracted a lot of attention, and several algorithms have been proposed [5, 6, 10, 16]. MDC is especially promising for video coding due to the very stringent delay requirement in many video applications [37]. Recently, the MD version of sampling [38] is a popular technique for the design of MD video coding. In [38], an MDC scheme is presented with pre- and post-processing stages. Redundancy is added by padding various numbers of zeros in one dimension DCT domain of each frame, and multiple descriptions are generated by subsampling zero padded frames. It is showed in [38] that the one-dimensional approach performs much better than two-dimensional padding techniques in [39], at a much lower computational complexity. However, in [38] through zero padding inside the frames, only the correlation of intra-frame is considered to improve side distortion, and the temporal correlation of inter-frame is neglected completely.

In this section, we attempt to design a more effective MD video coder based on pre/post-processing and subsampling [40]. In view of the different motion informa-

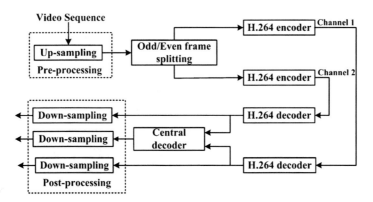

Fig. 4.33 Block diagram of the proposed scheme

tion between frames, the redundancy is added adaptively to make a better trade-off between the reconstructed quality and the compression efficiency. Consequently, the abrupt motion may result in worse side distortion so more redundancy is needed to guarantee the correlation between frames, while less or no redundancy is needed if the motion of inter-frame is smooth enough.

4.5.2   Proposed Scheme

Figure 4.33 illustrates our proposed scheme for MD video coding. In the preprocessing stage, the original video sequence is up-sampled to generate a new-length video with adaptively redundant frames. And then by means of odd and even frames, the new video sequence is divided into two descriptions, which can be compressed by any standard video codec. Here, the latest video coding standard H.264 is employed for a suitable comparison. In the post-processing, the decoded video stream is down-sampled to reconstruct original-length video, and error concealment method is used to estimate lost frames. The details of pre- and post-processing are showed in the following subsections.

4.5.2.1   The Preprocessing Stage

In terms of the principle of MDC, higher quality of side decoded video that will result from more correlations in descriptions for better error concealment is available, but more redundancy introduced will bring about lower efficiency to the central decoder. Obviously, it is a better solution that the redundancy added can make a trade-off between the reconstructed quality and the compression efficiency. As a result, in the preprocessing stage, the up-sampling with changeable rate is employed to introduce the adaptive redundancy. Since different motion appearance

Fig. 4.34 The flowchart of
up-sampling

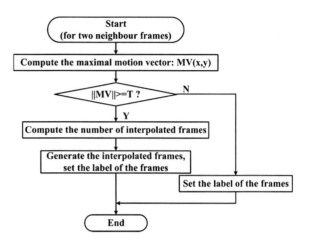

Fig. 4.34 The flowchart of
up-sampling

of inter-frames will affect the quality of side decoded video, the rate of up-sampling
is various according to the motion information between any two neighboring frames.
The obvious motion between the frames can result in more interpolated frames and
higher rate of up-sampling. On the other hand, if the motion information of the
inter-frame is very smooth, fewer or no redundant frames are needed. Such method
of up-sampling mainly aims to generate descriptions with smooth motion which
makes better evaluation of lost frames available at the side decoder.

In Fig. 4.34, the flowchart of up-sampling is shown step by step. For any two
neighboring frames, all the motion vectors for each macroblock are computed,
and the maximum can be obtained. Here it is denoted by $\|MV\|$ and $\|MV\| = \sqrt{x^2 + y^2}$ ((x, y) are the coordinates of the maximal motion vector). Then the
maximal motion vector is compared with the threshold T. If $\|MV\| < T$, the
motion between the two frames is considered smooth so no frames need to be
interpolated. Otherwise, redundant frames are needed. In view of the balance of
two channels, even frames are interpolated to maintain equal frame number of
two descriptions. Consequently, the number of interpolated frames is computed
by $2 \times [(\|MV\| / T - 1) / 2]$. In the end, the redundant frames can be generated
using the general algorithm of motion compensated interpolation, such as in [41].
Additionally, the label with one bit ("1" or "0") is set for each frame to distinguish
the original frame and interpolated one, then duplicated and transmitted on two
channels. Here, we assume label $= 1$ represents the original frame, and label $= 0$ is
the interpolated one.

4.5.2.2 The Post-processing Stage

In the post-processing stage, two situations for decoding exist, that is, the design of
central or side decoder.

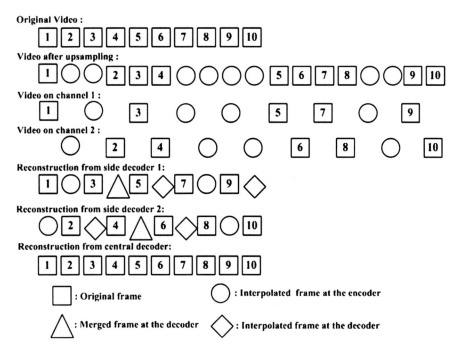

Fig. 4.35 A simple example for the pre- and post-processing

Since the two descriptions are generated by odd and even means, at the central decoder, the video streams from H.264 decoder can be interleaved and realigned in the same way to achieve the redundant video. According to the labels ("1" or "0"), the interpolated frames can be deleted, so the redundant video can be down-sampled to obtain the final reconstruction which has the same frame number with the original video sequences.

If only one channel works, the side decoder is employed, and four possibilities should be taken into account:

1. If the current label is "1" but its following label is "0," the represented frame is just the reconstructed one.
2. If the current label is "0" but its following label is "1," the represented frame is the interpolated frame, and it can be regarded as the reconstructed one.
3. If the current label is "0" and its following label is also "0," the continuous frames represented by "0" should be merged to a reconstructed frame.
4. If the current label is "1," and its following label is also "1," a new frame should be interpolated between the two frames denoted by "1."

In Fig. 4.35, a simple example illustrates the pre- and post-processing. The original video sequence has ten frames denoted by frame 1 to frame 10. After up-sampling, the redundant video has 18 frames. From the figure, we can see even frames are interpolated adaptively, such as two frames interpolated between frame 1

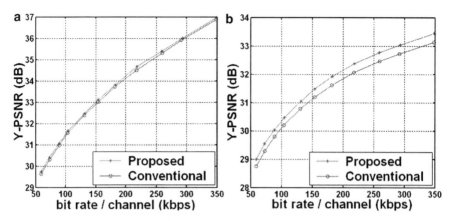

Fig. 4.36 Comparison for the test video "Coastguard.qcif." (**a**) Rate/central distortion performance; (**b**) Rate/side distortion performance

and frame 2, four frames interpolated between frame 4 and frame 5. After splitting by odd and even means, the generated descriptions are denoted by video on channel 1 and video on channel 2, and the labels are "101001101" and "011001101," respectively. When only channel 1 works, the reconstruction from side decoder 1 is achieved like the figure. The two interpolated frames between frame 3 and frame 5 will be merged into a new reconstructed one, while a new frame is interpolated between frame 5 and frame 7 to evaluate the lost frame 6. On the other hand, if two channels work, the lossless video may be obtained without the processing by H.264 codec.

4.5.3   Experimental Results

Here, there are mainly two experiments taken into account to present the efficiency of up-sampling in temporal domain. The first one shows the better performance of the proposed scheme than the conventional scheme without up-sampling in the preprocessing stage. In the second experiment, the advantage of the proposed scheme is illuminated compared with the up-sampling in the spatial domain.

The conventional scheme is similar with Fig. 4.33 but without up-sampling block. The standard test video "Coastguard.qcif" is used with 30 frames per second. For a fair comparison, the same mode and parameters are chosen in H.264 encoder and decoder [42]. Additionally, we also employ the same method of motion compensated interpolation.

In Fig. 4.36, at the almost same central distortion, the side distortion of the proposed scheme has 0.5 dB better than the conventional scheme. However, this is just a global comparison for the average of the whole video. In fact, some individual frames may achieve more advantages over the conventional schemes. Figure 4.37

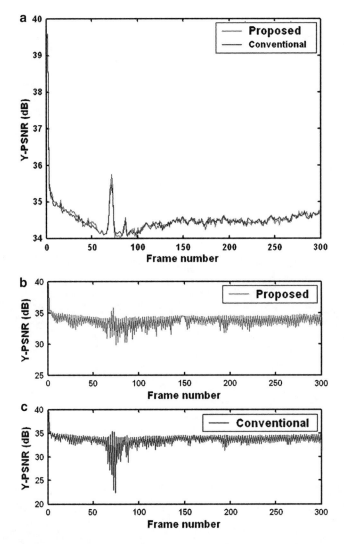

Fig. 4.37 Comparison for the test video "Coastguard.qcif." (**a**) Central PSNR values for each frame; (**b**) Side PSNR values for each frame

shows the central and side PSNR of each frame at the bit rate of 138 kbps achieved by the proposed and conventional schemes. From Fig. 4.37a, it can be seen that the central PSNR of the two compared schemes have almost the same performance. However, in Fig. 4.37b, the proposed scheme can perform obvious improvement in the side distortion around the frame number 70. From Fig. 4.38, 4.39, 4.40 and 4.41, the side reconstructed frames by the two compared schemes are presented to illustrate the efficiency of the proposed scheme.

Fig. 4.38 (**a**) The conventional scheme (Frame no.:70, Side PSNR: 26.267 dB). (**b**) The proposed scheme (Frame no.:70, Side PSNR: 31.352 dB)

Fig. 4.39 (**a**) The conventional scheme (Frame no.:72, Side PSNR: 22.999 dB). (**b**) The proposed scheme (Frame no.:72, Side PSNR: 31.681 dB)

Fig. 4.40 (**a**) The conventional scheme (Frame no.:74, Side PSNR: 22.435 dB). (**b**) The proposed scheme (Frame no.:74, Side PSNR: 26.698 dB)

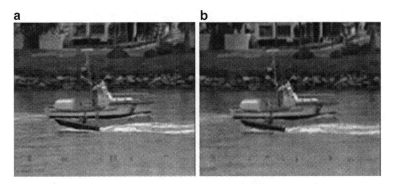

Fig. 4.41 (**a**) The conventional scheme (Frame no.:76, Side PSNR: 28.702 dB). (**b**) The proposed scheme (Frame no.76, Side PSNR: 31.075 dB)

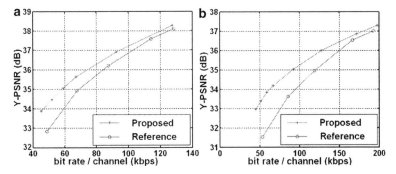

Fig. 4.42 Comparison for the test video "Foreman.qcif." (**a**) Rate/central distortion performance. (**b**) Rate/side distortion performance

To present the advantage over the scheme using up-sampling in spatial domain, the proposed scheme is compared with [38] in Fig. 4.42. For a fair comparison, the same code mode of H.264 is employed in the two compared schemes for the test video "Foreman.qcif." From Fig. 4.42, we can see better rate and central/side distortion performance achieved by the proposed scheme, especially at the lower bit rate.

4.5.4 Summary

An MD video coding scheme based on the pre- and post-processing has been developed in the section, without any modification to the source or channel codec. In view of the temporal redundancy and actual motion information, adaptive motion compensated interpolation has been accommodated in the proposed system to achieve better trade-off between the reconstructed quality and the compression efficiency. As a result, the proposed MD video coding scheme has demonstrated superior rate-distortion performance compared to the MD video coder in [38].

4.6 Priority Encoding Transmission Based MDC

4.6.1 Motivation

During the past years, several MDC algorithms have been proposed for the on–off channels. Based on the principle of MD scalar quantizer [29], an MD scheme for video coding is proposed in [43], while MD correlation transform is also employed to design motion-compensated MD video coding [44]. Although the above methods have shown good performance, they are incompatible with widely used standard codecs, such as H.26x and MPEG-x.

To overcome the limitation, subsampling technique is applied, such as the MD video coder based on spatial subsampling [38] and the MD video coder based on temporal subsampling [40]. Furthermore, a new approach to MDC is proposed in [45], suitable for block-transform coders, which are the basis of current video coding standards. In [46], multiple scalable descriptions are generated from a single SVC-compliant bit stream by mapping scalability layers of different frames to different descriptions. And the new schemes of MD video coding are also presented in [47, 48] based on H.264/AVC. In view of packet loss network, an unequal packet loss protection scheme is designed in [49] for robust H.264/AVC bit stream transmission, which can achieve higher PSNR values and better user perceived quality than the equal loss protection scheme. In [50], the proposed MD system uses an overdetermined filter bank to generate multiple descriptions and allows for exact signal reconstruction in the presence of packet losses, which is reported to be competitive compared with other spatial subsampling scheme.

For transmission over packet loss network, FEC-based multiple description (FEC-MD) is an attractive approach. The basic idea is to partition a source bit stream into segments with different importance, and protect these segments using different amounts of FEC channel codes, so as to convert a prioritized bit stream into multiple non-prioritized segments. However, this method currently is limited to the scalable video coders [51–53]. In [54], the scheme can be independent from any specific scalable application. However, as the important factor for the amount of added redundancy, the priority is not optimized to satisfy the channel characteristics.

Inspired by [54], in this section, we attempt to overcome the limitation of specific scalable video codec and apply FEC-MD to a common video coder [55], such as the standard H.264. According to different motion characteristics between frames, an original video sequence is divided into several subsequences as messages, so in each message better temporal correlation can be maintained for better estimation when information losses occur. Based on priority encoding transmission, unequal protections are assigned in each message. Furthermore, the priority is designed in view of packet loss rate of channels and the significance of bit streams.

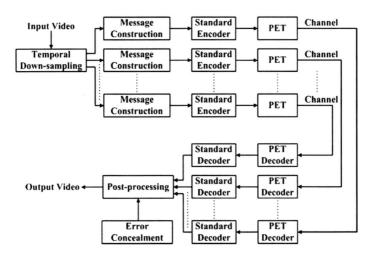

Fig. 4.43 Block diagram of our proposed scheme

4.6.2   Overview

Figure 4.43 illustrates our scheme, and a step-by-step recipe is explained as follows.

Step 1: Temporal Down-sampling

In this chapter, multiple descriptions can be generated using temporal down-sampling. Here, take two descriptions as a simple example. In the conventional method, odd and even frames can be separated to produce two descriptions. However, for the frames with high motion changing, simple splitting may result in difficult estimation of lost information at the decoder. Therefore, in the proposed scheme, these frames are duplicated in each description to maintain the temporal correlations when the original video is down-sampled.

For any two neighboring frames, the motion vector for each macroblock (MB) is computed, and the maximal motion vector (MV_x, MV_y) can be obtained. Here, $\|MV\| = \sqrt{MV_x^2 + MV_y^2}$. The change of $\|MV\|$ can be used as the measure to determine the motion between the frames. For any three neighboring frames denoted by $k, k-1$, and $k-2$, if $\|MV\|_{(k,k-1)} - \|MV\|_{(k-1,k-2)} > T$, high motion change is considered between frame k and $k-1$. For keeping temporal correlations between the frames, frame k and $k-1$ are duplicated in each description. Here, the threshold T is an experience value, which can be determined according to many experimental results.

Suppose in a video with ten frames, high motion exists between the fifth frame and sixth frame. As a result, two generated descriptions are as follows: Description 1 is organized by frame *1, 3, 5, 6, 7, 9*, and Description 2 is frame *2, 4, 5, 6, 8, 10*. It can be seen that frame *5* and *6* are duplicated in each description. At the same time, the serial number of the frames can be adopted to distinguish the position of the frames with motion changing, that is, the continuous frame sequence such as frame *5* and *6* can mean high motion occurs.

Step 2: Message Construction

In view of the motion characteristics between the frames, each description can be divided into messages at the position of high motion. In the above example, Description 1 can be divided into two messages, that is, frame *1, 3, 5* as one message and frame *6, 7, 9* as the other message. Similarly in Description 2, the two messages are frame *2, 4, 5* and frame *6, 8, 10*, respectively.

Message construction may lead to some improvements. Firstly, flexible group of picture (GOP) is available due to different message construction. The first frame in each message can be intra-encoded as *I* frame, and the encoding structure of GOP is chosen according to the length of the message. It is noted that the threshold value T can influence flexible GOP structure, because the length of each message may become longer with T increasing, which leads to the change of GOP structure. Next, unequal error protection can be applied to both levels of intra- and inter-message. Firstly, unequal amounts of FEC bytes can be assigned to each frame due to different significance of *I, P, B* frames, which can produce the intra-message unequal protection. Furthermore, different amounts of *I, P, B* frames exist in the distinct GOP, which can lead to the unequal protection on the inter-message level.

Step 3: Standard Encoder

Each message can be encoded to bit streams using current standard codec. Here, H.264 encoder is chosen, and obviously the proposed scheme is compatible with the standard codec. It is noted that in each message flexible group of picture (GOP) is employed which is helpful to refresh intra-frame adaptively. Compared with the uniform period of intra-frame, adaptive refreshment can keep up with the motion change between frames, so better temporal correlation can be maintained to achieve better error concealment if frame loss occurs in one message at the decoder.

Step 4: Priority Encoding Transmission (PET)

Priority encoding transmission is an algorithm that assigns unequal amounts of FEC bytes to different segments of the message according to specified priorities. Priorities are expressed by percentage of packets needed to reconstruct the original information. When the priority is high, corresponding message segment can be recovered using few packets received by the decoder. At the same time, low priority means that more packets are needed to recover the message segments. For the message segments with FEC, as long as the number of lost packets is less than or equal to the number of FEC bytes, the entire recover will be achieved [54].

Here, the message segments in each bit stream can be composed of three types, that is, *I* frames, *P* frames, and *B* frames after H.264 encoding. In view of different

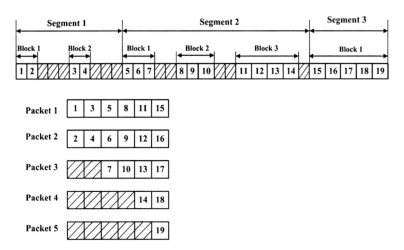

Fig. 4.44 An example of priority encoding transmission

significance, *I* frames have the highest priority, and *P* frames have higher priority than *B* frames. In this chapter, the packet loss rate of channels is also taken into account to design the priority, which will be discussed in Sect. 4.6.3 in detail. Figure 4.44 depicts a simple example of priority encoding transmission. For the message with 19 bytes, there are three segments whose priorities are 40%, 60%, and 100% respectively. Firstly, according to the demanded packet size 6 bytes and the priorities, each segment can be divided into blocks with appropriate FEC bytes. Here, since the priority of segment 1 is 40%, each block with 2 bytes is added by 3 FEC bytes. In the same way, each block with 3 bytes in segment 2 is protected by 2 bytes according to the priority 60%. It is noted that since the length of segment 2 is 10 bytes which cannot be divided averagely by 3 bytes, the length of block 3 has one more byte than the other two blocks. Additionally, for the priority 100% of segment 3, no FEC bytes are needed. Then the new message which includes the original data and FEC bytes will be mapped into five packets shown as Fig. 4.44. These packets can be transmitted to the receiver over channels.

Step 5: Decoder Design with Error Concealment

In the on–off channel environment, two cases for decoding should be taken into account, that is, the design of central decoder and side decoder. Since the two descriptions are generated by odd and even means, at the central decoder, the two video subsequences after standard decoding can be interleaved firstly. Then according to the serial number of the frames, the duplicated frames will be removed to obtain the central reconstruction. If only one channel works, the side decoder is employed to estimate the lost information. The widely used method of motion compensation interpolation (MCI) based on the piecewise uniform motion assumption is performed by bidirectional motion estimation, which may produce overlapped pixels and holes in the estimated frame.

For convenience, we denote by f the estimated frame between frame f_k and frame f_{k+1} and by $MV(\vec{p})$ the motion vector for the pixel location $\vec{p}$. To avoid the holes in the estimated frame, we can compute a preliminary reconstruction as background

$$f(\vec{p}) = \frac{1}{2}\left(f_k(\vec{p}) + f_{k+1}(\vec{p})\right). \tag{4.15}$$

Furthermore, the forward and backward motion compensation can be performed for frame f_{k+1} and f_k, respectively. To solve the overlapped problem of MCI, the mean values of overlapped pixels are adopted for motion compensation. Then the preliminary background may be replaced by the MCI-based reconstruction according to

$$f(\vec{p}) = \frac{1}{2}\left(f_k\left(\vec{p} - \frac{1}{2}MV(\vec{p})\right) + f_{k+1}\left(\vec{p} + \frac{1}{2}MV(\vec{p})\right)\right). \tag{4.16}$$

In packet loss network, due to both descriptions having received suffering from packet losses, only central decoder should be designed. After standard decoding, the two generated video subsequences are interleaved by odd and even means firstly to produce a video with redundant frames. At the decoder, the segments whose priorities are not higher than the fraction of packet received can be recover totally. Otherwise, the segment of higher priorities cannot remedy the error data due to packet loss, which may turn to frame loss. In this case, error concealment should be used to estimate the lost frames. For lost I frame or P frame within one message, the last I frame or P frame that has been decoded correctly can be adopted for forward prediction using motion compensation extrapolation. For lost B frame within one message, its forward and backward I frame or P frame can be used for bidirectional prediction using motion compensation interpolation. Lastly, the duplicated frames are removed to obtain the central reconstruction.

4.6.3 Design of Priority

In the algorithm of priority encoding transmission, the priority percent of segments in each message is a significant factor that can determine the amount of the FEC bytes added, so the design of priority aims to achieve better reconstruction at the cost of fewer FEC bytes. Therefore, we can assign the priority to each segment according to their contribution for the improvement of the message reconstruction. In order to estimate the contribution of the segment, a decoding process with error concealment is simulated at the encoder. To facilitate the following, some notations are defined in the following.

Let us assume I frame, P frame, and B frame are the three types of segments in the description. $PSNR(I)$ denotes the reconstruction quality of the message when only

I frame can be decoded correctly. For simplicity, the lost *P* or *B* frame can be reconstructed as the copy of *I* frame. $PSNR(I, P)$ then represents the recovery when both *I* and *P* frames can be received correctly. Here, the lost *B* frame can be estimated using motion compensation interpolation. And $PSNR(I, P, B)$ is the entirely reconstruction with no losses. Obviously, $PSNR(I, P, B) > PSNR(I, P) > PSNR(I)$. Therefore, we can consider the improvement due to *P* frame is $PSNR(P) = PSNR(I, P) - PSNR(I)$. In the same way, the improvement from *B* frame is $PSNR(B) = PSNR(I, P, B) - PSNR(I, P)$. $pri(I)$, $pri(P)$, and $pri(B)$ are the preliminary priorities of *I* frame, *P* frame, and *B* frame, respectively. As a result, we can compute the priorities:

$$pri(I) = k \times \frac{1}{PSNR(I)} \Big/ \left(\frac{1}{PSNR(I)} + \frac{1}{PSNR(P)} + \frac{1}{PSNR(B)} \right) \quad (4.17)$$

$$pri(P) = k \times \frac{1}{PSNR(P)} \Big/ \left(\frac{1}{PSNR(I)} + \frac{1}{PSNR(P)} + \frac{1}{PSNR(B)} \right) \quad (4.18)$$

$$pri(B) = k \times \frac{1}{PSNR(B)} \Big/ \left(\frac{1}{PSNR(I)} + \frac{1}{PSNR(P)} + \frac{1}{PSNR(B)} \right). \quad (4.19)$$

Here, the constant parameter *k* can be adjusted to satisfy the bit rate. The above equations provide the basic relationship between three priorities, so $pri(I)$, $pri(P)$, and $pri(B)$ can be computed from one to the other, that is,

$$pri(P) = pri(I) \times \frac{PSNR(I)}{PSNR(P)} \quad (4.20)$$

$$pri(B) = pri(I) \times \frac{PSNR(I)}{PSNR(B)}. \quad (4.21)$$

If the largest packet loss rate (*PLR*) of channels is taken into account and the acceptable lowest reconstruction quality is *PSNR*, the formulas can be modified as follows.

If $PSNR \geqslant PSNR(I)$, then the priorities can be updated as $pri(I) = 1 - PLR$, and $pri(P)$ and $pri(B)$ can be computed according to their relationship.

Similarly, if $PSNR \geqslant PSNR(I, P)$, then the priorities will be modified as $pri(I) = pri(P) = 1 - PLR$, and $pri(B)$ can also be computed from $pri(I)$.

If $PSNR = PSNR(I, P, B)$, that is, the entire recovery should be achieved, then $pri(I) = pri(P) = pri(B) = 1 - PLR$.

The design of priority needs the decoding process with error concealment which increases the encoding computational complexity to some extent. However, we use frame level based error concealment to lower the complexity. When computing $PSNR(I)$, frame duplication is a fast algorithm to reconstruct the lost frames. When computing $PSNR(I, P)$, the motion between frames is considered uniform, therefore, once motion compensation can interpolate multiple lost frames. When computing $PSNR(I, P, B)$, we can utilize the reconstructed reference frames in

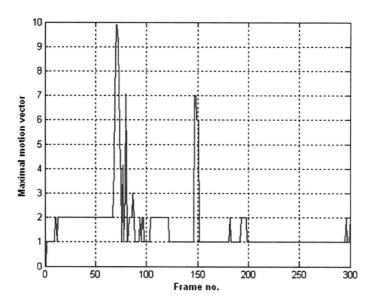

Fig. 4.45 $\|MV\|$s of maximal motion vector between frames

H.264 encoding process to reduce the complexity. Moreover, the decision of priority can be implemented offline which guarantees the real time of the whole system.

4.6.4   Experimental Results

In this section, the proposed scheme is tested using some standard video sequence in CIF-YUV 4:2:0 or QCIF-YUV 4:2:0 format. The frame rate is 30 fps. As for the video codec, we have employed H.264 encoder [42], and the software version is JM10.2. Firstly, we present the proposed message construction and the performance of flexible GOP. Next, the advantage of the proposed scheme exhibits compared with the equal protection scheme. Lastly, in view of different MD environments, that is, the on–off channel environment and packet loss network, the experiments are performed to evaluate the efficiency of the proposed scheme with respect to state-of-the-art methods.

4.6.4.1   Message Construction

Figure 4.45 shows $\|MV\|$s of maximal motion vectors for the standard video sequence "Coastguard.qcif." Here, the threshold $T = 1$. In the original video "Coastguard.qcif," according to the position of high motion 18 frames are duplicated, and then 13 messages are constructed in each description shown in Fig. 4.46.

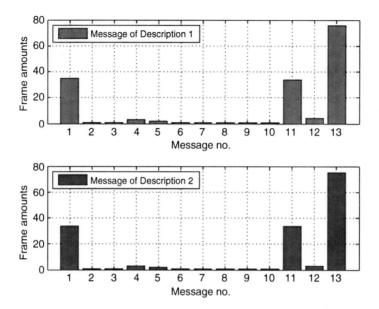

Fig. 4.46 Messages of each description

Table 4.6 The code structure of each description for "Coastguard.qcif"	Message no.	Frame amounts	Coding structure
	1	34	I-P-B-B- P-B-B . . .
	2	1	I
	3	1	I
	4	3	I-P-B
	5	2	I-P
	6	1	I
	7	1	I
	8	1	I
	9	1	I
	10	1	I
	11	34	I-P-B-B- P-B-B . . .
	12	4	I-P-B-B
	13	75	I-P-B-P-B . . .

According to the frame amounts of messages in Fig. 4.46, the coding structure for each description, that is, the coding type for each frame, is designed, as shown in Table 4.6. Table 4.6, shows the flexible GOP to satisfy the different messages. Furthermore, the frames with high motion are encoded as *I* frame, which may be assigned for important protection using PET algorithm.

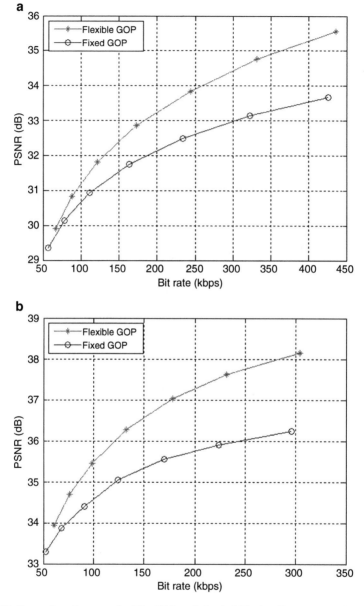

Fig. 4.47 Comparison between flexible GOP and fixed GOP: (**a**) Coastguard.qcif; (**b**) Fore-man.qcif

4.6.4.2 Flexible GOP

To substantiate the improvement of the proposed scheme with flexible GOP, the following experiment is performed. The first 100 frames of the standard video

"Coastguard.qcif" are selected to produce two descriptions directly by odd/even frame splitting. Then the generated descriptions are encoded by H.264 with flexible GOP and fixed GOP. Lastly, the same error concealment is applied to reconstruct the lost frames when only one description is received. Here, the flexible GOP is as Table 4.6 for "Coastguard.qcif," and the fixed GOP is I-P-B-B-P-B-B. From Fig. 4.47a, it can be seen that better rate-distortion performance is achieved by the flexible GOP than fixed GOP. Furthermore, in Fig. 4.47b, the standard video "Foreman.qcif" is also tested to obtain the same results.

4.6.4.3   Equal Protection Scheme Comparison

According to Fig. 4.46, the 300 frames of "Coastguard.qcif" can be split into two descriptions, and each description has 13 messages. The quantization parameters are chosen as QP (I: 25, P: 30, B: 30). And the coding structure of each message is shown in Table 4.6. After H.264 encoder, the total bit rate of all the messages is 124.59 kbps. The following experiments are based on such compressed bit streams.

After priority encoding transmission, the total bit rate of information data and FEC is 177.98 kbps for 300 frames. To make a fair comparison, the quantization parameters, coding structure, and error concealment are the same in the equal protection scheme. Figure 4.48 shows the performance of the proposed scheme against the equal protection over packet loss network at the same total bit rate. It is noted that in equal protection scheme, the same amounts of FEC bytes are assigned to the segments, which means the same priorities when using PET algorithm. From Fig. 4.48a, we can see that at the low packet loss rate (<30%), the performance of equal protection surpasses the proposed scheme, and the largest gap between the two schemes is less than 1 dB. However, at the packet loss rate 35%, the proposed scheme can degrade gracefully, while the equal protection has a sharp transition. Here, the largest gap that the proposed scheme surpasses the equal protection is about 6 dB. This is because in equal protection scheme the priorities of all the frames are 30%, that is, at the packet loss rate 35% almost all the frames cannot be decoded correctly, which results in the sharp degrade of the quality.

Figure 4.48b shows the performance of each frame at the packet loss rate 35%. Obviously, the proposed scheme has taken more advantages than the equal protection. We have also investigated the visual subjective quality of the proposed scheme compared with equal protection scheme. In Fig. 4.49, it can be seen that in equal protection scheme, substantial distortion exists from the 27th frame to the 30th frame, and the frame quality is significantly improved by the proposed scheme.

4.6.4.4   On–Off Channel Environment

In the following experiment, the rate-distortion performance is compared between the proposed with the scheme based on H.264 [48] in the on–off channel environment. For a fair comparison, the first 150 frames of "Mobile.cif" are selected, and

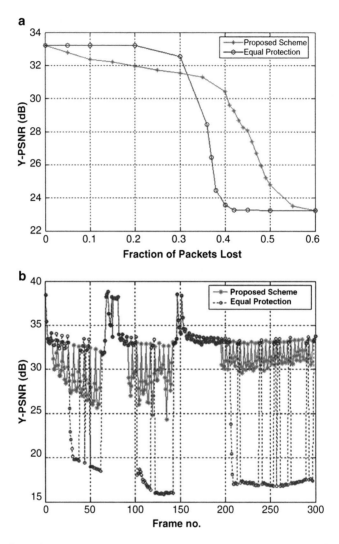

Fig. 4.48 Comparison between equal protection scheme and the proposed one for the video "Coastguard.qcif": (**a**) Average quality; (**b**) Quality of each frame

the coding structure is IPPP... without *B* frames. Figure 4.50 shows the central and side distortion performance of the proposed scheme against the scheme [48] at the same bit rate. From the figures, we can clearly see that the proposed scheme outperforms the tested scheme about 0.3–0.8 dB in side distortion and 0.7–1.8 dB in central distortion. From Fig. 4.50b, we can see that with the bit rate increasing PSNR gain becomes better due to better performance of error concealment at the decoder.

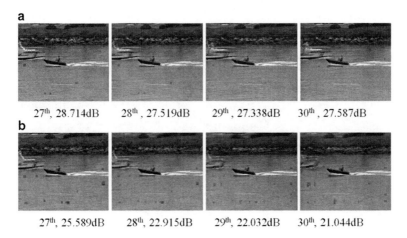

Fig. 4.49 Comparison of the visual subjective quality: (**a**) Proposed scheme, (**b**) Equal protection

Fig. 4.50 The rate-distortion performance of "Mobile.cif": (**a**) Reconstruction from one description; (**b**) Reconstruction from two descriptions

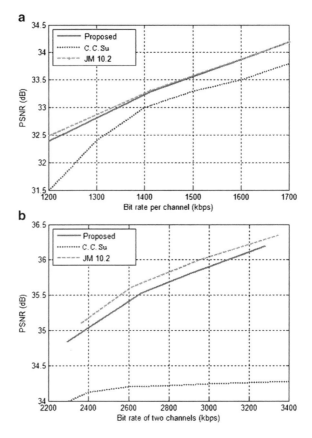

Fig. 4.51 The rate-distortion performance of "New.cif": (**a**) Packet loss rate 1%; (**b**) Packet loss rate 10%

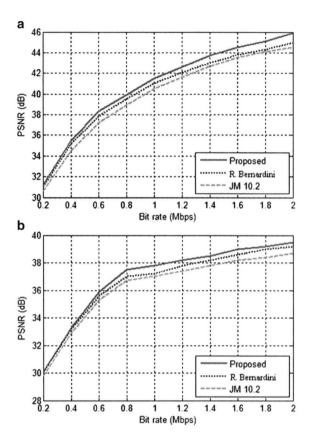

4.6.4.5   Packet Loss Network

We then evaluate the performance of the proposed video coding scheme compared with the MD system based on spatial subsampling [50] and other unequal protection scheme [49] in packet loss network.

Firstly, the 100 frames of "New.cif" are selected, and the GOP structure is *I BBBB P BBBB P BBBB P BBBB I* for a fair comparison. From Fig. 4.51, it can be seen for the packet loss rate 1% and 10%, that the proposed scheme performs better than the scheme in [50], which may result from better temporal correlation in the proposed scheme to estimate the lost information.

Next, the 100 frames of "Paris.cif" have been encoded in an IPBPB . . . structure for the comparison with the unequal protection scheme in [49]. The packet loss rate is tuned from 1% to 20%. Figure 4.52 shows the better performance of the proposed scheme than the compared one [49]. In [49], only three kinds of RS code are used for unequal protection, which may be a limitation of the performance.

Fig. 4.52 The performance
at different packet loss rates
for the video "Paris.cif"

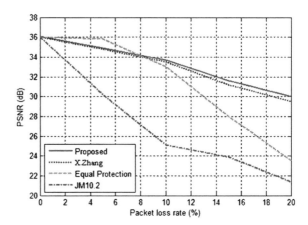

4.6.5 Summary

An MD video coding scheme using priority encoding transmission is presented in this chapter. Effective design of priority has been accommodated in the system to achieve better performance against the packet loss rate. For the message construction, different motion characteristics between frames are taken into account, so in each message, better temporal correlation can be maintained for better estimation when information losses occur. Furthermore, in view of the compatibility with the standard video codec, the proposed scheme may be a worthy choice for MD coding.

References

1. Goyal, V.K.: Multiple description coding: compression meets the network. IEEE Signal Process. Mag. **18**(5), 74–93 (2001)
2. Wang, Y., Orchard, M.T., Reibman, A.R.: Multiple description image coding for noisy channels by pairing transform coefficients. In: Proceedings of 1st Workshop on Multimedia Signal Processing, Princeton, pp. 419–424 (June 1997)
3. Srinivasan, M., Chellappa, R.: Multiple description subband coding. In: Proceedings of IEEE International Conference on Image Processing, Chicago, vol. 1, pp. 684–688 (Oct 1998)
4. Servetto, S.D., Vaishampayan, V.A., Sloane, N.J.A.: Multiple description lattice vector quantization. In: Proceedings of IEEE Data Compression Conference, Snowbird, pp. 13–22 (Mar 1999)
5. Servetto, S.D., Ramchandran, K., Vaishampayan, V.A., Nahrstedt, K.: Multiple description wavelet based image coding. IEEE Trans Image Process **9**(5), 813–826 (2000)
6. Tian, C., Hemami, S.S.: A new class of multiple description scalar quantizer and its application to image coding. IEEE Signal Process. Lett. **12**(4), 329–332 (2005)
7. Vaishampayan, V.A., Sloane, N.J.A., Servetto, S.D.: Multiple description vector quantization with lattice codebooks: design and analysis. IEEE Trans. Inf. Theory **47**(5), 1718–1734 (2001)
8. Bai, H., Zhao, Y., Zhu, C.: Optimized multiple description image coding using lattice vector quantization. In: IEEE International Symposium on Circuits and Systems, Kobe, vol. 4, pp. 4038–4041 (May 2005)

9. Tian, C., Hemami, S.S.: An embedded image coding system based on Tarp filter with classification. In: Proceedings of International Conference on Acoustics, Speech, Signal Processing, Montreal, vol. 3, pp. 49–52 (May 2004)
10. Tillo, T., Olmo, G.: A novel multiple description coding scheme compatible with the JPEG2000 decoder. IEEE Signal Process. Lett. **11**(11), 908–911 (2004)
11. Shapiro, J.M.: Embedded image coding using zerotrees of wavelet coefficients. IEEE Trans. Signal Process. **41**(12), 3445–3462 (1993)
12. Conway, J.H., Sloane, N.J.A.: Sphere Packings, Lattices and Groups, 3rd edn, pp. 108–117. Springer, New York (1998)
13. Nelson, M., Gailly, J.: The Data Compression Book, 2nd edn. M&T Books, New York (1995)
14. Bai, H., Zhu, C., Zhao, Y.: Optimized multiple description lattice vector quantization for wavelet image coding. IEEE Trans. Circuits Syst. Video Technol. **17**(7), 912–917 (2007)
15. Goyal, V.K., Kelner, J.A., Kovacevic, J.: Multiple description vector quantization with a coarse lattice. IEEE Trans. Inf. Theory **48**, 781–788 (2002)
16. Bai, H., Zhao, Y., Zhu, C.: Multiple description shifted lattice vector quantization for progressive wavelet image coding. In: IEEE International Conference on Image Processing, Atlanta, pp. 797–800 (2006)
17. Guionnet, T., Guillemot, C., Pateux, S.: Embedded multiple description coding for progressive image transmission over unreliable channels. In: Proceedings of IEEE International Conference on Image Processing ICIP'01, Thessaloniki, pp. 94–97 (2001)
18. Jiang, W., Ortega, A.: Multiple description coding via polyphase transform and selective quantization. In: Proceedings of SPIE International Conference on Visual Communications and Image Processing, VCIP'99, San Jose, pp. 998–1008 (1999)
19. Gavrilescu, A.I., Munteanu, A., Schelkens, P., Comelis,J.: Embedded multiple description scalar quantizer for progressive image transmission. In: Proceedings of International Conference on Acoustics, Speech, and Signal Processing, ICASSP'03, Hong Kong, vol. 5, pp. 736–739 (2003)
20. Zhao, D.Y., Kleijn, W.B.: Multiple-description vector quantization using translated lattices with local optimization. In: IEEE Global Telecommunications Conference, GLOBECOM '04, vol. 1, Dallas, Texas, pp. 41–45 (2004)
21. Conway, J.H., Sloane, N.J.A.: Fast quantizing and decoding algorithms for lattice quantizers and codes. IEEE Trans. Inf. Theory **28**(2), 227–232 (1982)
22. Wang, Y., Orchard, M.T., Vaishampayan, V., Reibman, A.R.: Multiple description coding using pairwise correlating transforms. IEEE Trans Image Process **10**(3), 351–366 (2001)
23. Zhong, X., Juang, B.-H.: Multiple description speech coding with diversities. In: Proceedings of IEEE International Conference on Acoustics, Speech, and Signal Processing, Orlando, vol. 1, pp. 177–180 (2002)
24. Tian, S., Rajan, P.K.: Multiple description coding using transforms and data fusion. In: Proceedings of International Conference on Information Technology: Coding and Computing, vol. 1, Las Vegas, Nevada, pp. 85–90 (2005)
25. Lin, C., Zhao, Y., Zhu, C.: Two-stage diversity-based multiple description image coding. IEEE Signal Process. Lett. **15**, 837–840 (2008)
26. Banister, B.A., Fischer, T.R.: Quadtree classification and TCQ image coding. IEEE Trans. Circuits Syst. Video Technol. **11**(1), 3–8 (2001)
27. Liu, Y., Oraintara, S.: Feature-oriented multiple description wavelet-based image coding. IEEE Trans Image Process **16**(1), 121–131 (2007)
28. Baccaglini, E., Tillo, T., Olmo, G.: A flexible R-D-based multiple description scheme for JPEG 2000. IEEE Signal Process. Lett. **14**(3), 197–200 (2007)
29. Vaishampayan, V.: Design of multiple description scalar quantizers. IEEE Trans. Inf. Theory **39**, 821–834 (1993)
30. Norkin, A., Gotchev, A., Egiazarian, K., Astola, J.: Two-stage multiple description image coders: analysis and comparative study. Signal Process. Image Commun. **21**, 609–625 (2006)

31. Tillo, T., Grangetto, M., Olmo, G.: Multiple description image coding based on Lagrangian rate allocation. IEEE Trans Image Process **16**, 673–683 (2007)
32. Zhang, Z., Zhu, C., Zhao, Y.: Two-description image coding with steganography. IEEE Signal Process. Lett. **15**, 887–890 (2008)
33. Bender, W., Morimoto, N., Lu, A.: Techniques for data hiding. IBM Syst. J. **35**, 313–336 (1996)
34. Boato, G., Carli, M., Conci, N., De Natale, F.G.B., Neri, A.: Improving perceptual quality of multiple description coding by data hiding. In: Proceedings of 3rd International Workshop Video Processing and Quality Metrics for Consumer Electronics, Scottsdale (2007)
35. Wu, D.C., Tsai, W.H.: A steganography method for images by pixel value differencing. Pattern Recognit. Lett. **24**, 1613–1626 (2003)
36. Salama, P., Shroff, N.B., Delp, E.J.: Error concealment technique for encoded video streams. In: Proceedings of International Conference on Image Processing (ICIP 1995), Washington, DC, vol. 1, pp. 9–12 (Oct 1995)
37. Wang, Y., Reibman, A.R., Lin, S.: Multiple description coding for video delivery. Proc. IEEE **93**(1), 57–70 (2005)
38. Wang, D., Canagarajah, N., Redmill, D., Bull, D.: Multiple description video coding based on zero padding. In: Proceedings of the 2004 International Symposium on Circuits and Systems 2004, ISCAS '04, Vancouver, vol. 2, pp. 205–208 (May 2004)
39. Gallant, M., Shirani, S., Kossentini, F.: Standard-compliant multiple description video coding. In: IEEE International Conference on Image Processing, Thessaloniki (Oct 2001)
40. Bai, H., Zhao, Y., Zhu, C.: Multiple description video coding using adaptive temporal sub-sampling. In: International Conference on Multimedia and Expo (ICME), Beijing, pp. 1331–1334 (July 2007)
41. Wei, L., Zhao, Y., Wang, A.: Improved side-information in distributed source coding. In: International Conference on Innovative Computing, Information and Control, Beijing, vol. 2, pp. 209–212 (Aug 2006)
42. JVT-G050. ITU-T Recommendation and Final Draft International Standard of Joint Video Specification (ITU-T Rec. H.264 | ISO/IEC 14496-10 AVC), 2003
43. Vaishampayan, V., John, S.: Balanced interframe multiple description video compression. In: International Conference on Image Processing (ICIP), Kobe, vol. 3, pp. 812–816 (Oct 1999)
44. Reibman, A.R., Jafarkhani, H., Wang, Y., Orchard, M.T., Puri, R.: Multiple description coding for video using motion compensated prediction. In: International Conference on Image Processing (ICIP), Kobe, vol. 3, pp. 837–841 (Oct 1999)
45. Conci, N., De Natale, F.G.B.: Multiple description video coding using coefficients ordering and interpolation. Signal Process. Image Commun. **22**(3), 252–265 (2007)
46. Abanoz, T.B., Tekalp, A.M.: SVC-based scalable multiple description video coding and optimization of encoding configuration. Signal Process. Image Commun. **24**(9), 691–701 (2009)
47. Radulovic, I., Frossard, P., Wang, Y.K., Hannuksela, M.M., Hallapuro, A.: Multiple description video coding with H.264/AVC redundant pictures. IEEE Trans. Circuits Syst. Video Technol. **20**, 144–148 (2010)
48. Su, C.C., Chen, H.H., Yao, J.J., Huang, P.: H.264/AVC-based multiple description video coding using dynamic slice groups. Signal Process. Image Commun. **23**(9), 677–691 (2008)
49. Zhang, X., Peng, X.: An unequal packet loss protection scheme for H.264/AVC video transmission. In: Proceedings of IEEE ICOIN, Chiang Mai, Thailand, pp. 1–5 (Jan 2009)
50. Bernardini, R., Rinaldo, R., Tonello, A., Vitali, A.: Frame based multiple description for multimedia transmission over wireless networks. In: Proceedings of 7th International Symposium on WPMC, Abano Terme, vol. 2, pp. 529–532 (July 2004)
51. Mohr, A.E., Riskin, E.A., Ladner, R.E.: Graceful degradation over packet erasure channels through forward error correction. In: Proceedings of Data Compression Conference, DCC '99, Snowbird , pp. 92–101 (Mar 1999)
52. Stankovic, V., Hamzaoui, R., Xiong, Z.: Packet loss protection of embedded data with fast local search. In: Proceedings of IEEE ICIP, Rochester (Sept 2002)

53. Dumitrescu, S., Wu, X., Wang, Z.: Globally optimal uneven error-protected packetization of scalable code streams. IEEE Trans. Multimed **6**, 230–239 (2004)
54. Leicher, C.: Hierarchical encoding of MPEG sequences using priority encoding transmission (PET). Technical Report Tr-94–058, ICSI (Nov 1994)
55. Bai, H., Zhao, Y., Zhang, Z.: Standard-compliant multiple description video coding over packet loss network. EURASIP J. Adv. Signal Process **2010**, Article ID 987164, 9 p (2010)

Chapter 5
Algorithms of DVC

In traditional video coding system, such as standard MPEG serials and H.26x algorithms, it is the encoder that performs inter-frame prediction to exploit the correlation among successive frames. Since predictive coding makes use of motion estimation, the complexity of the encoder is typically 5–10 times more than that of the decoder. This case is desirable for the applications where video is compressed once and decoded many times, as in broadcasting. However, some new friendly uplink communication applications including mobile camera phones and sensor network cameras may require low-complexity encoders. DSC and DVC provide theory foundations for easy encoding; thus, they can meet the demand of friendly uplinking multimedia services.

In recent years, we have proposed several new DVC frameworks. The property of low-complexity encoding is still preserved. Next, our researching work will be introduced one by one in detail.

5.1 Wyner-Ziv Method in Pixel Domain

5.1.1 Motivation

DSC refers to the dependent sources coding with dependence only accessible at decoder. Theories of Slepian-Wolf [1] and Wyner-Ziv [2] state that we can get almost the same compression performance using dependences only at decoder or at both encoder and decoder. These theoretical bases for DSC and DSC give us support for simplifying the encoder.

DVC is born with DSC's application in video coding. Generally, DVC consists of a quantizer following a lossless Slepian-Wolf codec. But in the present DVC schemes, such as those in [3, 4], only SQ is used, although Rebollo-Monedero et al. [5] point that LVQ be optimal, and the Slepian-Wolf codec of [3, 4] are based on a trellis and Turbo coding, respectively.

H. Bai et al., *Distributed Multiple Description Coding*,
DOI 10.1007/978-1-4471-2248-7_5, © Springer-Verlag London Limited 2011

In this section, we propose a new DVC framework where two LVQ (lattice vector quantization) and a rate-variable LDPC (low-density parity-check) are exploited. In both LVQ and LDPC, we use the frame interpolated from the decoded as the side information. Because of LVQ's exploitation of correlation of source and the better error-correcting capacity of LDPC, the proposed system achieves more than 1 dB improvement in PSNR than the referenced. Meanwhile, the property of low-complexity encoding is still preserved.

5.1.2 Overview

In the framework, we attempt to set up our DVC based on LVQ and LDPC. LVQ, as a special vector quantization, can offer better coding performance compared with SQ [6]. And LVQ's superiority over general VQ is that its index of codebook and its decoding can be computed according to the regular algebraic structure of lattices. Also, because of fast encoding and decoding algorithm such as in [7], LVQ can be easily used without heavy computation. But the problem from pure LVQ is its large index. So, in our scheme, a so-called LVQ with side information is exploited. In this method, only a difference vector is used to represent a set of lattice points, so the index of LVQ can be compressed again besides the compression in pure LVQ itself. Servetto [8] and Liu and Xiong [9] first propose this idea in theory, but they do not apply it to real signal processing.

And also, we use side information to help the reconstruction of pure LVQ. Because of the dependence between main and side information, this reconstruction is reasonable. And the regular structure of lattice makes this reconstruction convenient.

Additionally, a rate-variable LDPC (RV-LDPC) is used to act as Slepian-Wolf codec. LDPC is the most suitable candidate for DSC, and now some rate-fixed LDPC has been exploited in DSC [1, 2]. But in practice, the dependence of main information and side information is not known at encoder. So, the rate-fixed LDPC is not enough. Then, we exploit a rate-variable LDPC to meet the varying dependence in video frames. We use feedback and CRC (cyclic redundancy check) to a mother LDPC and send its parity bits in stages on demand from decoder. The rate-variable LDPC in [10] requires sending partial information, which is different from ours.

5.1.3 The Proposed Coding Framework

The proposed framework is shown is Fig. 5.1. It is mainly based on the coding architecture of [11]. But there are differences, such as we replace Turbo coding with LDPC and SQ with LVQ; the other contribution is that we use side information for the reconstruction of pure LVQ.

The system consists of intra-frame encoder and inter-frame decoder. To odd frame, X_{2i-1} and X_{2i+1}, conventional intra-frame coding and decoding methods

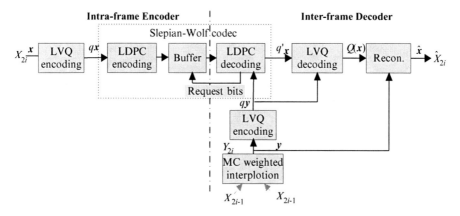

Fig. 5.1 The proposed DVC framework in pixel domain

can be used. As in [11], for simplicity, we view X_{2i-1} and X_{2i+1} *that* are decoded perfectly. While to even X_{2i}, its coding process is: at encoder, the adjacent pixels are grouped into vector x, and x is quantified by a pair of lattice vector quantizers. Then, the difference symbol of two lattice quantization, q_x, is encoded by Slepian-Wolf encoder. All parity bits are stored in buffer and ready to be sent on decoder's demands.

At decoder, firstly, an interpolation (or motion-compensation interpolation) is implemented from X_{2i-1} and X_{2i+1}, and we get side information Y_{2i}. Next, Y_{2i} is quantified by two LVQ same as encoder's and get q_y. Using q_y and the received parity bits, LDPC decoding is implemented to recovery q_x and LVQ decoding recovery $Q(x)$. Finally, y is used to reconstruct x, and the final reconstruction, $\hat{x}$, is achieved.

With a pair of lattice quantizer and LDPC, we can get better efficiencies than that with SQ and Turbo coding of [11]; on the other hand, LVQ based on fast algorithm will not bring much complex encoder than SQ, and the complex motion estimation is omitted from encoder, so, our system has also low-complexity encoder.

Next, we will describe the coding details in our scheme.

5.1.4 Implementation Details

5.1.4.1 LVQ Coding

The pure LVQ means that an input vector x is coded by an index of the lattice point $Q(x)$, nearest to x. We use the fast algorithm to get it. While, LVQ coding with side information is shown in Fig. 5.2, where $Q(x)$ and $Q_1(x)$ are called the lattice point and sub-lattice point for x, respectively. The coding processing is as follows:

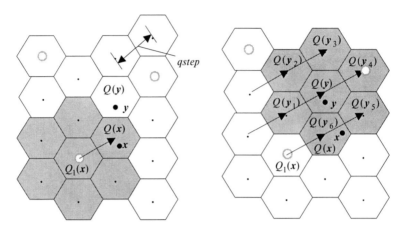

Fig. 5.2 Encoding (*left*) and decoding (*right*) of LVQ with side information

1. Getting $Q(x)$ and $Q_1(x)$, respectively, then the difference vector $T(x)$, $T(x) = Q(x) - Q_1(x)$, and sending $T(x)$ to decoder
2. Getting $Q(y)$ and finding all lattice points around $Q(y)$, that is, $\{Q(y_1), Q(y_2), \ldots, Q(y_{N-1})\}$, as shown in Fig. 5.2, where N is the number of difference vector
3. Computing $S_i = T(x) + Q(y_i)$ $(i = 1, \ldots, N)$, where $Q(y_N) = Q(y)$
4. Determining the sub-lattice points from S_i $(i = 1, \ldots, N)$; apparently, only $Q_1(x)$ is a sub-lattice point, so we get $Q_1(x)$
5. Finding $Q(x)$, that is, $Q(x) = T(x) + Q_1(x)$

Apparently, $T(x)$ represents a set of lattice points. So, if only $T(x)$ is sent to decoder, compression can be achieved. The compression rate is determined by N.

5.1.4.2 Reconstruction

In reconstruction, if y is in the region indicated by $Q(x)$, y is taken as the reconstruction, that is, $\hat{x} = y$, otherwise, the nearest to y in the lattice region as the restored.

5.1.4.3 Slepian-Wolf Codec

Here, for a rate-fixed LDPC, storing all of its parity bit in a buffer, then based on the demand from decoder, sending partial parity bits stage by stage until MPA (message-passing algorithm) converges. Here, MPA is for the received parity bits and q_y, which is similar to a noisy version of q_x through a binary symmetric channel.

5.1.5 *Experimental Results*

The experiment condition is similar to [11], and only luminance of even frames is counted. Lattice A_2 is used, and we try $N = 7, 13, 31, 61, 217$ (the bits per pixel is 1.5, 2, 2.5, 3, and 4, respectively), respectively. The experiments include:

1. Comparing LVQ + LDPC with SQ + LDPC to check the function of LVQ
2. Comparing the proposed system with the video standard coding H.263+, (I-B-I-B and I-I-I-I)

The results are shown in Fig. 5.3; from the results, we can see that LVQ performs better than SQ in our DVC, and the whole system has about 1 dB improvement in PSNR compared with [11], and the proposed system has 4–8 dB PSNR higher than H.263+ intra-frame encoding. Besides, for Foreman sequences with high motion, the technology makes the performance better than that has no MC.

In Fig. 5.4, we show the comparison for interpolated and reconstructed frames. The rate for a pixel is 2.5 bits, and average sequence bit rate is 240 kbps. From Fig. 5.4, we can see that our coding scheme can produce acceptable reconstructed image even in the case of simple average interpolation, and it can improve the reconstructed quality even if interpolation fails (such as in the case of Fig. 5.4).

5.1.6 *Summary*

In this section, we use lattice vector quantization and channel coding rate-variable LDPC to distributed video coding. Experiment results show that our system has higher performance than that based on Turbo and SQ, and its PSNR is higher than H.263+ intra-frame encoding and decoding. But the expected results have not yet been achieved, and the future work will be developed at the high-dimensional lattice vector quantization and transform-domain distributed video coding.

5.2 Wyner-Ziv Method in Wavelet Domain

5.2.1 *Motivation*

Recently, among some practical DVC systems [3, 10, 11], Anne Aaron and Bernd Girod have provided an easy scheme with low-complexity encoder [10, 11]. They encode the key frames in conventional intra-frame mode. To other frames, the Wyner-Ziv ones, a Slepian-Wolf codec based on Turbo coding is used. Anne's scheme [4] is built on DCT domain; while, it has been proved that DWT can overcome the "block effect" brought by block-wise DCT and achieve better coding performance in image coding. So, in our scheme, we want to set up our DVC scheme

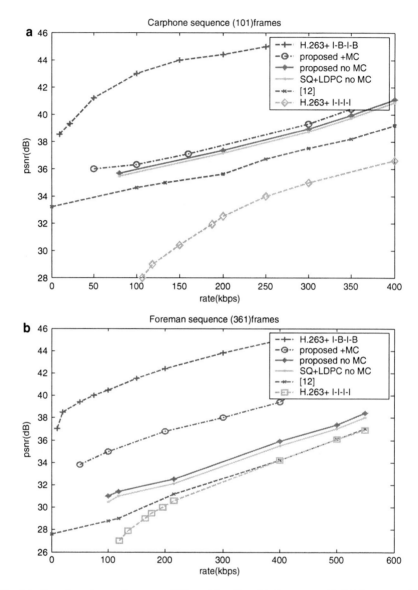

Fig. 5.3 Rate-distortion performance of Wyner-Ziv video. (**a**) Carphone.qcif, (**b**) Foreman.qcif

in wavelet domain. Additionally, we use a pair of lattice vector quantization (LVQ) to subtract the dependence between wavelet coefficients, which is different from [3, 10, 11] based on scalar quantization (SQ).

Side information is important in DVC. The more dependent side information is, the less burden Slepian-Wolf codec will have, and less bits are sent. Now, to get better side information, the average and motion-compensated interpolation are both presented [11], but in these interpolations, the side information is only built on past

Fig. 5.4 Reconstructed frames of Foreman.qcif. (**a**) Original, (**b**) interpolated average, (**c**) reconstructed average, (**d**) interpolated MC, (**e**) reconstructed MC

or future frames without any information from current frame. Then, here, we present using partially decoded current frame to refine the reconstruction and update the side information. Also, we give a new search strategy, modified weighted minimum absolutes distance (MWMAD), for motion searching of vector reconstruction of wavelet coefficients. This is the so-called motion compensation refinement, which was first presented in [12], but we extend it to wavelet domain and get partial decoding from frequency band instead of bit plane. And because of the dependence between coefficients of different frequency bands, our method seems more valid. Additionally, this refinement at decoder is different from the idea of [3, 13] which is based on a helpful "hash" from encoder. Our method is based on decoded current frame, which does not bring increase of bit rate naturally.

We propose a distributed video coding (DVC) paradigm based on lattice vector quantization in wavelet domain. In this framework, we use a fine and a coarse lattice vector quantizer to wavelet coefficients, and the difference of two lattice quantizers is coded by Turbo encoder. At decoder, side information is gradually updated by motion-compensated refinement. The refinement is built on partially decoded current frame, and we give its matching strategy. Due to the refinement, burden of Turbo encoding is cut down, bit rate is saved, and the reconstruction is improved to some degree. Also, because of the exploitation of dependence between wavelet components, our system can offer better rate-distortion performance than pixel domain.

5.2.2 Overview

Here, the proposed framework is mainly based on the coding architecture of [11]. But there are differences, such as we replace DCT with DWT and SQ with LVQ; the other contribution is that we extend the motion compensation refinement concept of pixel domain to wavelet domain and give the new searching strategy for vector reconstruction.

As shown in Fig. 5.5, the system consists of intra-frame encoder and inter-frame decoder. To odd frame, X_{2i-1} and X_{2i+1}, conventional intra-frame coding and decoding methods can be used. While to even X_{2i}, coding process is as follows: after DWT, its wavelet coefficients are grouped into vectors and quantified by a

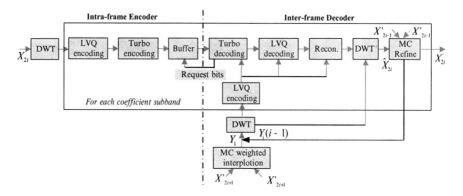

Fig. 5.5 The proposed DVC framework in wavelet domain

pair of lattice vector quantizers. Then, for each wavelet sub-band, Turbo encoder codes the symbol sequence of the difference vector. The parity bits from RCPT (rate compatible punctured turbo code) are stored in buffer and ready for to be sent on decoder's demands. At decoder, the side information is refined gradually. That is, firstly, Y_1 is decomposed by DWT, and its lowest frequency coefficients are used as side information for the lowest frequency symbol of X_{2i}. Then, organizing the restored lowest frequency and the other frequency coefficients from Y_1, after DWT^{-1}, we get partially decoded current frame $\hat{X}_{2i}$ for the first time. Based on $\hat{X}_{2i}$, the restored X'_{2i-1} and X'_{2i+1}, an MC refinement is implemented, and we get more accurate X'_{2i}. Then, for second frequency, X'_{2i} is used as side information Y_2. So, side information is updated, and the second Wyner-Ziv decoding starts. This refinement is used for reconstruction step by step until all frequency coefficients are decoded. Here, inner loops are developed in refinement for side information.

With DWT and a pair of lattice quantizers, we can get as good as or better efficiencies than that with DCT and SQ; additionally, the refined reconstruction brings about the quality enhancement for reconstructed frame, and meanwhile, the burden of Turbo coding is cut down due to updated side information. Besides, lattice vector quantization based on fast algorithm [7] will not bring much higher complexity than [11] at encoder, though the refinement will make decoder more complex because of motion searching, but this will not affect the friendly uplink application.

5.2.3 The Proposed Coding Framework

5.2.3.1 Lattice Vector Quantization to Wavelet Coefficients

In LVQ, an input vector x is coded by an index corresponding to the lattice point $Q(x)$nearest to x [7], while, in LVQ encoding, we mainly base the scheme as: LVQ with side information in [8, 9]. But in [8] and [9], this scheme is only studied in theory. To every input vector x, we use a pair of lattice quantizers with the same dimension, that is, the fine quantization $Q(.)$ and the coarse $Q_1(.)$ Then, send the symbol of difference vector, $T(x) = Q(x) - Q_1(x)$, to decoder. If x and side information y exist in an identical coarse Voronoi cell, then $Q(x)$ can be computed losslessly at decoder. But with above method, we can only get $Q(x)$, an approximation to original x. So, in reconstruction, we use side information again and take the nearest to side information in Voronoi cell indicated by $Q(x)$ as the final reconstruction. Here, the difference vector represents a set of lattice points so it gets compression again [8, 9].

In our scheme, A_2 lattice is used to quantify wavelet coefficients. Then in each frequency sub-band, two-dimensional vectors are formed and quantified with 2^{M_k} quantization level (here, the quantization level is determined by the number of difference vector of two lattice quantizers), where $2^{M_k} \in \{0, 8, 16, 32, 64, 128, 256, 512, 1024\}$. Here, $2^{M_k} = 0$ means no bits are sent, and the according coefficients from side information are used as the reconstruction. In fact, the above quantization accords to 0, 1.5, 2, 2.5, 3, 3.5, 4, 4.5, 5 bits per pixel, respectively, and the according bit rate of LVQ, the number of difference vector, is $N = 7, 13, 31, 61, 127, 217, 469, 919$.

The combination of above quantization determines the quantization for whole image. To determine the combination, we trained several sequences and tried all possible combinations certainly with a goal, that is, to decrease quantization level with frequency level increases. We record rate-distortion points and finally get "optimal" quantization label in Fig. 5.6, and we find this combination improves PSNR, where we adopt three-level wavelet decomposing, and the data in Fig. 5.6 show the number of bits that every pixel is quantified in its frequency sub-band.

5.2.3.2 Motion-Compensated Weighted Interpolation

Here, the MC weighted interpolation is only used to get the original side information Y_1 for the lowest frequency sub-band. In DVC, averaged interpolation is an easy and practical method, but it does not give more consideration to motion area. In our system, Y_1 is from motion-compensated interpolation, but we use an easy weighted interpolation for multiply frames to overcome the overlapped and vacancy in interpolated frame. The process is, firstly, fixing frame X'_{2i+1}, for a block b_{2i+1} in X'_{2i+1}, we search over X'_{2i-1} and find a most matched block b_{2i-1} and its motion vector (v_x, v_y) in it, then for the interpolated frame Y_{2ib}, in the position $(v_x/2, v_y/2)$, we get interpolated block $(b_{2i+1} + b_{2i-1})/2$; second, fixing X'_{2i-1}, for block b'_{2i-1} in X'_{2i-1}, searching the matched block b'_{2i+1} in X'_{2i+1}, we get the interpolated block $(b'_{2i-1} + b'_{2i+1})/2$ in the same position of interpolated frame Y_{2if}; finally, the interpolated side information is taken as:

$$y_{2i} = \alpha x'_{2i-1} + \beta x'_{2i+1} + \gamma y_{2ib} + \theta y_{2if} \qquad (5.1)$$

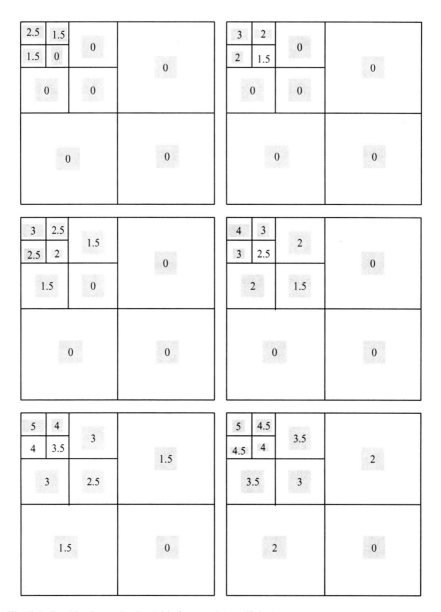

Fig. 5.6 Combined quantization table for wavelet coefficients

where y_{2i}, x'_{2i+1}, x'_{2i-1}, y_{2ib}, y_{2if} are the pixels of Y_{2i}, X'_{2i+1}, X'_{2i-1}, Y_{2ib}, Y_{2if}, respectively, and α, β, γ, θ are the weighted coefficients accordingly. Here, we assume the motion between adjacent frames is uniform.

5.2.3.3 Motion-Compensated Refinement

Intuitively, the more information about current frame we can get, the more accurate reconstruction and side information can be achieved. The goal of motion-compensated refinement is to get more accurate reconstructed and side information from decoded current frame. This is different from the original MC interpolation in Sect. 5.2.3.2 where decoder does not have any information about current frame. Here, we use the decoded lower frequency coefficients and the other higher coefficients from side information to restore a partially decoded frame. And with this decoded current frame and its past and previous, we get a better reconstruction, which will, in turn, make the side information more accurate for next frequency and consequently, cut down the burden of Turbo decoding in higher frequency because of improved side information.

It is necessary to introduce refinement to decoded Wyner-Ziv frame. This is because in Wyner-Ziv coding process, firstly, Turbo decoder corrects quantified side information and gets the almost error-free symbol of quantization ($P_e \leq 10^{-3}$). Then, in reconstruction stage, decoder recoveries the quantization, that is, if side information is in the same bin indicated by corrected quantization sequence, then side information is taken as the reconstruction, otherwise, the nearest to side information in the bin is the reconstructed. This reconstruction process limits the maximum distortion from side information but brings other distortion because of inaccurate side information. So, it is necessary to introduce refinement to decoded frame.

The refinement works when the difference between the reconstructed and side information is bigger than the threshold [6], that is,

$$\sum_{(m,n)\in\text{Block}} |\widehat{x}_{2i}(m,n) - y_{2i}(m,n)| \geq \tau \qquad (5.2)$$

where (m, n) is the coordination of pixel.

Then, what we should do is to find a more accurate block to compensate this block. This is another contribution of this section. We base our block searching on a matching criterion:

$$MWMAD = MAD(x, y) \times |\hat{C}_{2i} - C_{\text{ref}}| / K \qquad (5.3)$$

where $\hat{C}_{2i}$ and C_{ref} are both wavelet coefficients in the same sub-band as just decoded sub-band. While $\hat{C}_{2i}$ is from $\hat{X}_{2i}$, and C_{ref} is from the reference frame. K is the number of same quantization output when quantify $\hat{C}_{2i}$ and C_{ref} using LVQ. This criterion, on one hand, limits the block which has wavelet coefficients far away from the reconstructed in reference frame and, on the other hand, promotes the blocks which have the most number of quantization output equal to that of $\hat{X}_{2i}$. The search is to find the minimal $MWMAD$ to compensate the reconstructed frame $\hat{X}$. Ascenso et al. [12] adopt a *WMAD* (weighted mean absolute difference) which only considers *MAD* of reference frames and the quantization results but not the reconstruction. Here, the reference frames refer to the past, future, and the bidirectional searched frames in the past and future frames [12, 14].

5.2.4 Experimental Results

We do comparison experiments as follows for two QCIF video sequences: the first 101 frames in Foreman and Carphone. We only count the luminance of even frames assuming its frame rate is 15 frames per second. RCPT is from [15], and the experiment condition is similar to [11]. In our experiments, we use biorthogonal 9/7 wavelet transform. The rate-distortion is plotted in Fig. 5.7; meanwhile, the inter-frame coding efficiency, I-B-I-B, of standard H.263+ is shown. And "pixel domain" refers to the coding system based on LVQ but only omitting the wavelet transform and motion compensation refinement. The partial MR means that only reconstruction is refined, and full MR is implemented to both reconstruction and side information.

From the results, we can see our DVC of wavelet domain achieves up to 1 dB improvement in PSNR than [11] of DCT, that is, with DWT and lattice quantization, we can get better results. These can be seen in both Foreman and Carphone sequences. Meanwhile, the wavelet transform brings better efficiency than pixel domain, though the improvement is not evident in Carphone sequence.

As for the motion-compensated refinement technology, we can see it undoubtedly brings improvements to reconstruction of DVC system, especially in lower rate and high motion sequence. Besides, if the refinement is used to side information, it will cut down the burden of Turbo coding and, consequently, bring up to 20 Kb saving in 250 Kb/s.

From Fig. 5.8, we can see the reconstructed image is good and the refinement makes the motion area clear in eyes and mouth of Foreman.

5.2.5 Summary

We implemented a new LVQ-based DVC system with motion-compensated refinement in wavelet domain [16]. Our system outperforms the referenced. But the refinements are not so useful in less motion sequences, and experiment results do not reach expectation. Also, there are some drawbacks, for example, the rate is determined by feedback, and the scalable nature of wavelet transform is not included. Maybe these will be included in future work.

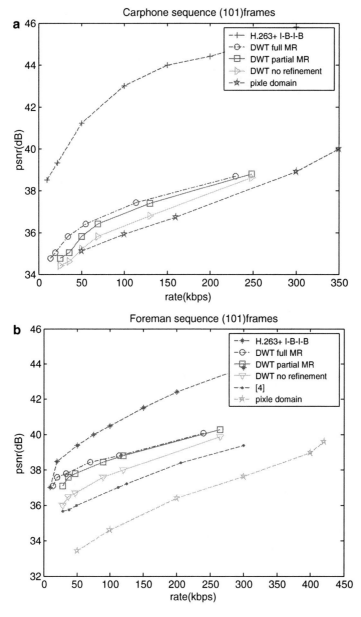

Fig. 5.7 Rate-distortion performance of Wyner-Ziv video for luminance. (**a**) Carphone.qcif, (**b**) Foreman.qcif

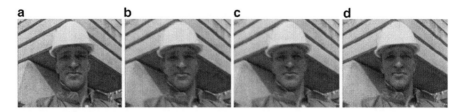

Fig. 5.8 Visual quality. (**a**) Original, (**b**) MC interpolated, (**c**) reconstructed (40 kbps), (**d**) refined reconstruct(40 kbps)

5.3   Residual DVC Based on LQR Hash

5.3.1   Motivation

Generally in DVC system, for the Wyner-Ziv frames, the quantized pixels or transform coefficient X is channel encoded, and only the parity bits P are transmitted. At the decoder, the error-correcting decoding using the parity bits P and SI Y is implemented to recover X. The reconstruction is to recover the original pixels or coefficients with the help of SI generated by the decoded key frames.

As the estimation to the main source, SI Y is very important in DSC and DVC. Generally, the more dependent Y is, the less parity bits and the higher compression as well as the better reconstruction can be achieved. Among some methods, hash-based SI is the most attractive method [13]. The main idea is that except the Wyner-Ziv bits, the encoder also sends some representing information on encoding to assist the motion estimation. Because the hash bits take more information about current frame, the hash-based motion estimation is more accurate than that without hash. On the other hand, the hash-based DVC is enhanced at the cost of hash bits sent. Therefore, the hash should be compressed efficiently. Specially, in [13], the compression of hash bits is based on the entropy code, so the hash bit rate is $R(h) \geq H(h)$. Martinian et al. [17] propose use of the LQR frame to generate efficient hash. The LQR hash refers to the low-quality version of the current Wyner-Ziv frame. LQR hash is coded by the prediction coding similar to the DPCM/DCT with 0-motion-searching and coarse quantization. Just because the temporal dependence is exploited, the bit rate of LQR hash approaches, ideally, the conditional entropy $R(h) \geq H(h|Y)$, and better rate-distortion can be obtained. But, the LQR-based method in [17] has an apparent disadvantage. For example, LQR hash bits and Wyner-Ziv bits are two different streams compressed by 0-motion H.264 and Wyner-Ziv codec, respectively, for the same frame. So there is redundancy between LQR and Wyner-Ziv bits especially at high bit rate.

On the other hand, it is shown that residual DVC can give better performance than pure pixel DVC [18]. Residual DVC means Wyner-Ziv encoding the residual $D = W - W_{re}$, where W_{re} is a simple estimation to W and should be accessible both at the encoder and the decoder. $D_y = Y - W_{re}$ is used as SI Wyner-Ziv decoding.

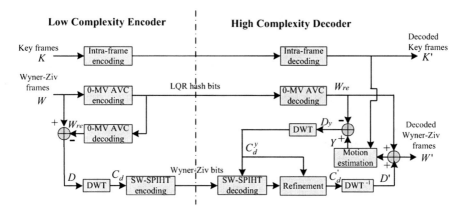

Fig. 5.9 Proposed residual DVC based on LQR

Finally, W_{re} is added to obtain the recovered W'. In residual DVC, W_{re} acts as second SI accessible at the encoder. Because there are dependences between W_{re} and W, coding the residual brings improvement to pure DVC.

Motivated by the above analysis, in this section, some improvements will be given to the residual DVC based on LQR hash [19]. We firstly propose to use the decoded LQR hash as W_{re} for residual DVC. Each decoded LQR frame is just the coarse version of each W, so it is dependent on W. Also, SW-SPIHT is used to the residual D, which can further decrease the spatial redundancy in residual frame. Our contributions mainly include (1) combining the residual DVC with LQR hash to improve the rate-distortion performance, (2) exploiting SW-SPIHT to the residual, and (3) refining wavelet coefficients by SI.

In order to improve the rate-distortion performance of current DVC, this section presents a residual DVC based on low-quality reference (LQR) hash compressed by 0-motion H.264/AVC. SW-SPIHT (Slepian-Wolf set partitioning in hierarchical trees) is applied to the residual between Wyner-Ziv frame and the decoded LQR hash, which exploits the temporal and spatial correlations so improves the coding efficiency. At the decoder, the decoded LQR is used for more accurate motion estimation and better side information. And a refinement reconstruction with side information is proposed for better SPIHT decoding. The experimental results indicate the proposed scheme achieves better rate-distortion performance than current literatures. Meanwhile, no complex motion estimation is used at the encoder; thus, the easy encoding property of DVC is still preserved.

5.3.2   The Proposed Coding Framework

The proposed scheme is shown in Fig. 5.9. To the key frames, the H.264/AVC intra-frame encoding and decoding is implemented. While to the Wyner-Ziv frames, the low-complexity encoding and high-complexity decoding are implemented.

5.3.2.1 Low-Complexity Encoding

The encoder generates two kinds of bit streams for a Wyner-Ziv frame. One is the bit stream from LQR hash, that is, the bit stream from 0-motion H.264/AVC with coarse quantization. LQR encoding does not use any computational motion estimation, so it has low complexity. And for the sake of low-complexity encoding, the optimization to rate-distortion is omitted from the 0-motion H.264/AVC program.

The other bit stream, the Wyner-Ziv bits, is from the residual DVC. That is, the encoder first generates W_{re} from the 0-motion decoding; D is decomposed by discrete wavelet transform (DWT). Then, the wavelet coefficient C_d is encoded by SW-SPIHT encoding, and the outputted forms the so-called Wyner-Ziv bits.

SW-SPIHT encoding consists of DWT with SPIHT and channel encoding, so the complexity is similar to the intra-frame encoding. These above mentioned bring low-complexity encoding to the whole system.

5.3.2.2 High-Complexity Decoding

At the decoder, the decoded LQR is first used to do motion estimation to generate Y, which is explained in the Sect. 5.3.2.4. Then, the difference $D_y = Y - W_{re}$ is decomposed by a DWT similar to the encoder. The wavelet coefficient C_d^y of D_y is used as SI for SW-SPIHT decoding and the refinement process; consequently, the decoded $C_d{}'$ is achieved. Next, the inversed DWT is implemented, and the difference pixel D' is obtained. Finally, let $W' = W_{re} + D'$, then Wyner-Ziv frame is reconstructed. Note that the computational motion estimation and iterated channel decoding bring high-complexity decoding to DVC, though they do not influence the easy encoding property.

5.3.2.3 SW-SPIHT Codec

SW-SPIHT stands for the set partition in hierarchical trees (SPIHT) based on the Slepian-Wolf theory [18]. The main idea of SW-SPIHT builds on the fact that the SPIHT information is similar when two images are similar. So, SPIHT information can be compressed further by the lossless Slepian-Wolf model. The detail of SW-SPIHT can be found in [20].

5.3.2.4 Refinement to the Wavelet Coefficient

After SW-SPIHT decoding, SPIHT stream is recovered completely; the wavelet coefficients are refined based on the formula

$$C_d' = \begin{cases} v_{\max}, & \text{if } C_d^y \geq v_{\max} \\ C_d^y, & \text{if } C_d^y \in (v_{\min}, v_{\max}) \\ v_{\min}, & \text{if } C_d^y \leq v_{\min} \end{cases} \tag{5.4}$$

where C_d' is the final wavelet coefficient value after refinement; $v_{\max}$ and $v_{\min}$ are the possible maximal and minimal values of wavelet coefficient if SPIHT decoding is implemented to all BPs (assuming m, $m > n$). There are two reasons that this refinement gives improvement: one is that the recovered n BPs take some information of C_d, which will correct the noisy BPs of C_d^y and limit the distortion from C_d^y; the other is that some additional information from $m - n$ BPs of C_d^y is added to the recovered n BPs, which compensates the reconstruction of C_d from n BPs.

5.3.2.5   Motion Compensation Based on LQR Hash

The LQR-based motion compensation consists of two steps as following. Firstly, the motion estimation is implemented to find the best matched block and the corresponding motion vector. Specially, let $L_t(i, j)$ denote the value of the pixel at row i and column j of the decoded LQR in time t and let $R_t(i, j)$ denote the corresponding pixel in the referenced frame. Then the motion vector for the block at (a, b) is

$$\text{MAD}(a, b) = \arg\min_{dx, dy} \sum_{j=0}^{7} \sum_{i=0}^{7} |L_t(a + i, b + j) - R_t(a + i + dx, b + j + dy)| \tag{5.5}$$

where $dx \in [-8, 8]$ and $dy \in [-8, 8]$, and the decoded previous frame is used as the referenced frame. Secondly, we use the weighted average value of LQR and the matched block to generate the compensated block. That is,

$$\text{block}_{\text{comp}} = \alpha \times \text{block}_{\text{matched}} + (1 - \alpha) \times \text{block}_{\text{LQR}} \tag{5.6}$$

where $\text{block}_{\text{matched}}$ is the matched block searched for the block $\text{block}_{\text{LQR}}$ at (a, b) of LQR frame. α is an experimental value in $[0, 1]$.

5.3.3   Experimental Results

One hundred luminance frames of 15 Hz QCIF sequences *Foreman* and *Hall* are tested to evaluate the performance of DVC codec proposed. Meanwhile, constant decoded video quality for all key and Wyner-Ziv frames is considered in Table 5.1,

Table 5.1 Combined quantization in residual DVC

	Foreman					Hall				
	Q1	Q2	Q3	Q4	Q5	Q1	Q2	Q3	Q4	Q5
QP	41	36	32	26	20	40	33	29	24	19
BP	2	3	4	5	6	2	3	4	5	6

where QP value means the quantization chosen in JM9.0 for key frames and the quantization of Wyner-Ziv frame is chosen by the number of BP. The optimized combination quantization of five rate-distortion points Q1, Q2, Q3, Q4, and Q5 is shown.

Firstly, the PSNR of the reconstructed video with GOP 8 is shown in Fig. 5.10. The comparison experiments also include the non-residual DVC with LQR moving the subtraction operation of Fig. 5.1, and the results of residual DVC in [18] are compared.

Compared with the non-residual DVC, the proposed DVC gives 1.2–5.8 dB improvement. This improvement originates from the fact that the residual scheme can make use of second SI at the encoder [18]. When compared with the best results of [18], the proposed scheme obtains 1.2–3 dB improvements for *Foreman* sequence. This is because of the efficient hash and SW-SPIHT, which exploit the temporal and spatial correlation in of residual frames. In addition, compared with intra-frame coding of H.264/AVC, the proposed scheme has up to 6 dB enhancement in PSNR. However, there is still a gap from the state-of-the-art inter-frame coding of H.264/AVC.

The PSNR temporal evolution data is also plotted for Q1, Q2, Q3, Q4, and Q5 in Fig. 5.11, where the decoded video has acceptably constant quality for both the high and low motion sequences because of the optimized combination quantization.

Secondly, we change GOP size to obtain different rate-distortion curve in Fig. 5.12. It is shown that the bigger GOP does improve the rate-distortion when motion is low, as for *Hall* sequence. However, for high motion sequence *Foreman*, the rate-distortion curve is degressive with the GOP size. This is because the SI becomes bad with the GOP size especially for the high motion sequences.

5.3.4 Summary

In this section, a novel residual DVC based on the LQR of H.264/AVC is presented. This scheme benefits from the residual coding and the efficient LQR hash based motion compensation. It is the SW-SPIHT encodes the residual between Wyner-Ziv frame and a decoded LQR. The decoder recovers the Wyner-Ziv frame using decoded LQR and the motion-compensated SI. The experimental results show the scheme proposed has comparable rate-distortion performance, though the additional subtraction operation and decoding of LQR give some computation to the encoder.

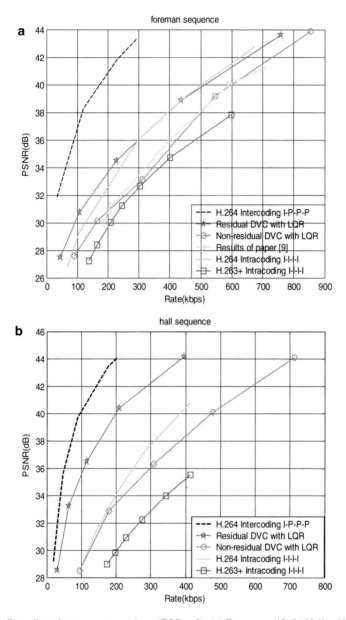

Fig. 5.10 Rate-distortion curve comparison (GOP = 8). (**a**) Foreman.qcif; (**b**) Hall.qcif

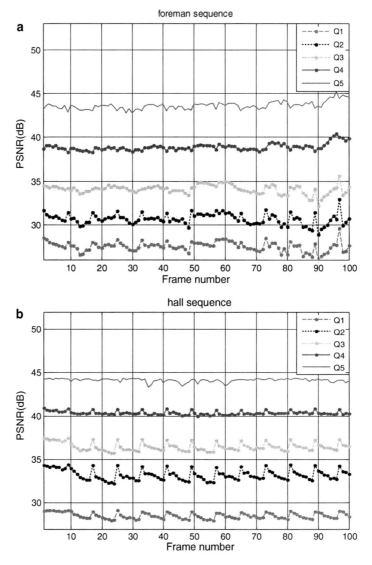

Fig. 5.11 Temporal evolution curve for all distortion points (GOP = 8). (**a**) Foreman.qcif, (**b**) Hall.qcif

5.4   Hybrid DVC

5.4.1   *Motivation*

Generally, the current DVC schemes are generalized as two approaches, including pixel-domain DVC and transform-domain DVC. Compared to the former, the latter

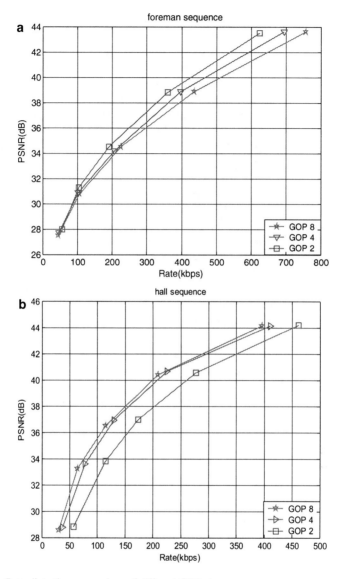

Fig. 5.12 Rate-distortion comparison of different GOP size

uses a transform-domain Wyner-Ziv codec instead of the pixel-domain one. For example, some transform-domain Wyner-Ziv codecs [21, 22] applied discrete cosine transform (DCT) to exploit spatial correlation within a frame, but the selection of the combined quantization for DCT coefficients bands is an arduous task. Anne Aaron [18] proposed a residual DVC to compress the residual frame between the current frame and a reference frame through pixel-domain Wyner-Ziv codec.

Due to the exploitation of the temporal correlation between the current frame and the reference frame at the encoder, residual DVC achieves almost the same rate-distortion performance as DCT-domain DVC. Meanwhile, the residual DVC overcomes the difficulty of the combined quantization selection. However, there is still some spatial correlation remaining in residual frames in [18]. The rate-distortion performance should be enhanced further if a proper transform coding with easily combined quantization methods is adopted to the residual frame. In this section, a wavelet-domain Wyner-Ziv codec with SPIHT is applied to the residual frame, which exploits the temporal and spatial correlation at the encoder simultaneously. Meanwhile, SPIHT brings convenience for the combined quantization of wavelet coefficients.

On the other hand, the current transform-domain Wyner-Ziv codec assumes the temporal correlation between the source to be encoded and its side information to be spatially stationary. In other words, different temporal correlation on the spatial location is negligible. Though the block-based intra-mode decision in pixel domain [23, 24] is proposed to classify the temporal correlation on spatial location, there is still much need to exploit intra-mode decision to the transform-domain. In our work, a mode decision based on temporal and spatial correlation is also proposed. When the estimated temporal correlation on the spatial location is weak, we use intra-SPIHT coding on the corresponding wavelet block (WB); otherwise the inter-mode coder SW-SPIHT is adopted.

Because of the combination of residual coding, SW-SPIHT coding and the intra-mode decision technique, the proposed DVC is named hybrid DVC (HDVC). The experimental results show HDVC achieves up to 4.1 dB improvement in PSNR than pure SW-SPIHT, 3.2 dB improvement than residual DVC, and 3 dB than the latest DCT-domain DVC of DISCOVER [21] with some neglectable complexity. Besides, the intra-mode decision offers up to 2.1 dB improvement at high motion area.

5.4.2 The Proposed Coding Framework

The framework of the proposed HDVC is shown in Fig. 5.13. Compared to the current DVC schemes, our contributions mainly focus on the following: (1) wavelet-domain Wyner-Ziv codec is applied on WBs instead of frames to provide some conveniences for temporal and spatial correlation analysis; (2) instead of original frames, the residual frame is used to construct WBs and analyzed to exploit the temporal and spatial correlation; (3) an intra-mode decision of wavelet domain is conducted to each WB to exploit different temporal and spatial correlation; (4) the intra-mode decision strategy based on temporal and spatial criteria is given in [25].

5.4.2.1 Wavelet-Domain Wyner-Ziv Codec Design for Residual Frames

Residual DVC had been proven to have the same performance as the DCT-domain DVC due to the exploitation of temporal correlation at the encoder [18]. Specially,

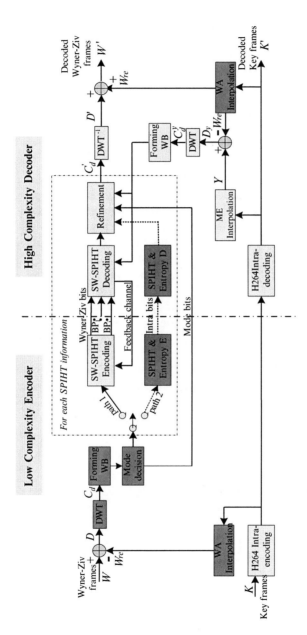

Fig. 5.13 The proposed HDVC framework

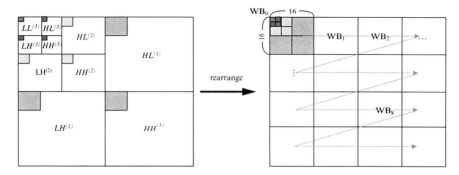

Fig. 5.14 WBs are rearranged and scanned in row-by-row

the frame W_{re}, the simple estimation to the current frame W, acts as the reference frame at both encoder and decoder. However, there is still some spatial correlation in the residual frame, so we propose a wavelet-domain Wyner-Ziv to the residual frames to extract the temporal and spatial correlation simultaneously at the encoder. The reference frame W_{re} is obtained by the weighted average (WA) interpolation:

$$W_{re} = \alpha K'_j + \beta K'_{j+1} \tag{5.7}$$

where K'_j and K'_{j+1} are the previous and next decoded key frames; $\alpha = 1 - l/g$, $\beta = 1 - \alpha$, where l is the number of frames between the current frame and the previous key frame K'_j in the same group of picture (GOP), g is the number of frames in a GOP.

At the encoder, the residual frame $D = W - W_{re}$ is decomposed by discrete wavelet transform (DWT) and the wavelet coefficients C_d are outputted.

At the decoder, the residual frame $D_y = Y - W_{re}$ is decomposed by the same DWT and the resulting coefficients C_d^y are generated. Here, Y is the more accurate estimation to the current frame and is generated by motion-estimated (ME) interpolation [18, 21] of key frames.

5.4.2.2   Intra-Mode Decision Strategy for WBs

In this section, WB is the basic coding unit. Typically, C_d and C_d^y are partitioned into 16×16 cross-scale WBs as in Fig. 5.14. In each WB, there are four 2×2 coefficients vectors from $LL^{(3)}$, $HL^{(3)}$, $LH^{(3)}$, and $HH^{(3)}$; three 4×4 from $HL^{(2)}$, $LH^{(2)}$, and $HH^{(2)}$; three 8×8 from $HL^{(1)}$, $LH^{(1)}$, and $HH^{(1)}$.

In Fig. 5.13, there are two encodings, intra-SPIHT and SW-SPIHT, to be determined for each WB. The encoding selection of each WB depends on the correlation derived from the temporal and spatial analyses. As a low encoding complexity scenario is targeted, a strategy which is easily implemented and capable of inferring the correlation between the current WB and its side information is needed. Here, the WB colocated at C_d^y is used as the side information for the current WB at C_d.

Based on the low frequency energy E_{LL} of current WB to be encoded, the temporal criterion is calculated as:

$$E_{LL} = \sum_{i=1}^{N_{LL}} (C_i^{LL})^2 \tag{5.8}$$

where C_i^{LL} is the ith coefficient in $LL^{(3)}$ band, N_{LL} is the total number of coefficients in $LL^{(3)}$, and $N_{LL} = 4$.

Meanwhile, based on the variance of high frequency coefficients of current WB, the spatial criterion is calculated as:

$$\sigma^2 = \frac{1}{N_h} \sum_{i=1}^{N_h} |C_i^h|^2 - \left(\frac{1}{N_h} \sum_{i=1}^{N_h} C_i^h \right)^2 \tag{5.9}$$

where C_i^h is the ith coefficient in all high frequency bands, N_h is the total number of coefficients in high frequency bands, $N_h = 12$.

There are two cases that the intra-SPIHT is used to a WB. In the first case of $E_{LL} \geq T_1$, the temporal correlation between current WB and its side information is assumed weak. That is, because E_{LL} collects most of the energy of WB, and the greater E_{LL} means the greater difference between the current frame W and the referenced frame W_{re}. While W_{re} is interpolated by the key frames with zero-motion vector. Then, it is likely that the correlation with Y interpolated by key frames with non-zero-motion vectors at the decoder is weak. So the correlation between current WB and its side information is weak. The second case occurs when $T_2 \leq E_{LL} < T_1$ and $\sigma^2 \leq T_3$. In this case the low frequency coefficients collect most of energy and the high frequency coefficients are spatially concentrated on small values so the intra-SPIHT coding is suited. Otherwise in the case of $E_{LL} < T_2$, the temporal correlation is inferred as strong, so SW-SPIHT is used. Here, T_1, T_2, and T_3 are the predetermined thresholds by experiments.

At the encoder, according to the intra-mode decision, two kinds of bit streams, the Wyner-Ziv bits and the intra-bits, are formed respectively by path 1 and path 2 as depicted in Fig. 5.13. The Wyner-Ziv bits consist of the syndrome bits of SW-SPIHT encoding. The intra-bits refer to the SPIHT information bits compressed by entropy coding. In our work, different SPIHT information streams in each bit-plane are encoded, respectively. In other word, the tree distribution information, the significant information, the refinement information, and the sign information are formed respectively by a row-by-row scanning among the blocks with the same mode. Each SPIHT information stream is compressed either by entropy coding or by SW coding with low-density parity-check accumulate (LDPCA) [26]. LDPCA with 396 nodes is adopted in our work. In the case of the sequence length less than 396, the padding zeros are applied. The details of SW-SPIHT for WBs are referred to in [27]. The binary mode bits are also encoded with entropy and sent to the decoder.

At the decoder, the bit streams are recovered either by LDPCA decoding or entropy decoding. The decoding selection depends on the decoded mode bits.

In addition, refinement process effectively reconstructs the current WB with side information WB at C_d^y. Next, the recovered coefficients C_d' are arranged and the residual frame D' is generated by inversed DWT. Finally, we have the recovered pixels from the residual frame and the reference frame as follows:

$$W' = D' + W_{re}. \tag{5.10}$$

5.4.3   Experimental Results

Experiments are conducted to the luminance component of standard QCIF@15 fps (frame per second) sequences. Five different DVC schemes are compared, including HDVC with intra-mode proposed, HDVC without intra-mode, pure SW-SPIHT DVC, the residual DVC, the DCT-domain DVC. Figures 5.15 and 5.16 show the results.

First, compared with the pure SW-SPIHT results computed based on [27], the proposed HDVC obtains up to 4.1 dB for *Hall* sequence. While compared with residual DVC results, which are computed based on [18], the improvement is up to 3.2 dB. These improvements originate from the fact that the hybrid scheme effectively employs some temporal and special correlation simultaneously at the encoder. Besides, compared with the latest DCT-domain DVC [1] results obtained from DISCOVER (www.discoverdvc.org), the proposed HDVC obtains up to 3 dB improvement for *Hall* sequence. For high motion sequence *Foreman*, there is only up to 0.9 dB improvement because the temporal correlation is weak.

Second, with the intra-mode decision, the evident quality improvement is achieved especially in the high motion frames. In Fig. 5.16, the intra-mode decision contributes up to 2.1 dB improvement in PSNR in high motion case.

In addition, compared with intra-frame coding of H.264/AVC, the proposed scheme has up to 7 dB enhancement in PSNR. However, there is still a gap from the state-of-the-art inter-frame coding of H.264/AVC.

5.4.4   Summary

In this section, an efficient hybrid DVC with intra-mode decision is presented to improve the rate-distortion performance of current DVC. This scheme benefits from the combination of residual coding, SW-SPIHT coding, and intra-mode decision strategy. It achieves more evident improvement than the pure SW-SPIHT, residual DVC, and the latest DCT-domain DVC of DISCOVER. The encoding of HDVC mainly consists of SPIHT, intra-mode decision, and LDPCA encoding. Thus, the proposed scheme avoids the complex motion estimation and preserves the low-complexity encoding similar to the intra-frame coding. While compared to the referenced DVC, our HDVC has a little more complex encoding due to

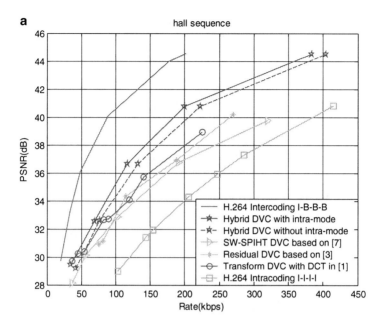

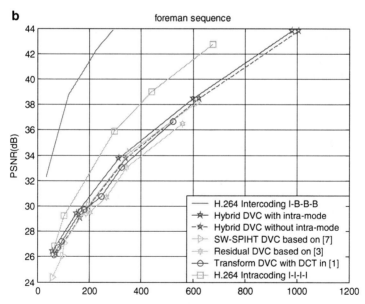

Fig. 5.15 Rate-distortion comparison when GOP = 8

the combining of mode decision and the subtraction operation, though they are neglectable. The proposed scheme is promising in the low-complexity encoding applications such as mobile cameras, wireless low-power surveillances.

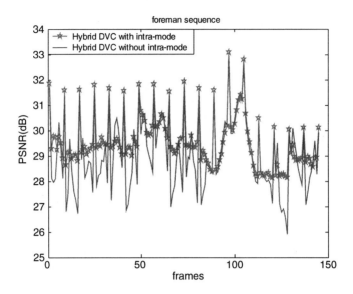

Fig. 5.16 Frames quality comparison when GOP $= 8$ and bit rate $= 166$ kbps

5.5   Scalable DVC Based on Block SW-SPIHT

5.5.1   Motivation

Scalability is important in many applications, such as to a set of heterogeneous mobile receivers having varying computational and display capabilities and/or channel capacities. Only some tentative schemes are proposed for scalable DVC, such as in [28–30]. And these schemes are built on a layered video framework in which a standard coded video (such as H.26L) is treated as a base layer. These frameworks have limited bit rate to be decoded. Meanwhile, the incomplete intra-frame encoding with motion compensation at encoding at base line is still adopted, which will influence the property of easy encoding. Besides, the disadvantage of fragile to lossy channel because of prediction coding still exists at base layer.

This section presents a scalable DVC scheme without requiring layered coding. This scheme inherits main attributes of DVC, namely the property of easy encoding and the robustness, while adding scalability as an additional feature. The scheme is based on a so-called block SW-SPIHT, and the binary motion searching is explored at decoder with the help of a rate-variable "hash" from encoder. Experiment results show our system has higher PSNR than the pixel-domain DVC at high bit rate. What is more, the SNR-scalability is achieved.

5.5.2 Overview

In this section, we will give more consideration to scalable DVC and try to preserve property of easy encoding and robustness [25]. We explore a complete intra-frame encoding model based on block SW-SPIHT to Wyner-Ziv frames. Like SPIHT, our block SW-SPIHT has the embedded bit stream. And this embedded bit stream has more flexibly truncated rates than layered coding. The complete intra-frame encoding has more robustness. We still base our DVC on Griod's framework (i.e., the even frames are encoded as Wyner-Ziv and the odd is key one, and also a Slepian-Wolf codec with feedback as in [13] and [31]) because of its convenience but adopt an embedded bit stream. Tang et al. [32] use SPIHT to distribute hyperspectral imagery and show better performance than intra-frame SPIHT, which give us light in thinking. We extend their idea of SW-SPIHT to wavelet block and develop a so-called block SW-SPIHT. Additionally, a binary motion searching (BMS) at decoder with rate-adaptive "hash" is proposed to block SW-SPIHT. The rate-adaptive "hash" is based on some parity bits from a rate compatible channel coding. This is different from the fixed-rate "hash" in [13]. Here, it is noted that "hash" refers to some representation information on encoding. And "hash" is sent to decoder to convey some helpful information of encoding and to help the motion searching at decoder.

5.5.3 The Proposed Coding Scheme

The proposed scalable DVC framework is depicted in Fig. 5.17, where "Generating WBs" refers to rearranging the wavelet coefficients and generating the cross-scale wavelet blocks (WB), as shown in Fig. 5.2. "Block SPIHT encoding" is the SPIHT for WB, which will be described in Sect. 5.5.3.2. "AC encoding" and "AC decoding" means the arithmetic encoding and decoding, respectively. And "SW encoding" refers to the Slepian-Wolf encoding based on a rate compatible channel coding with feedback. Meanwhile, buffer is used to store the parity bits of channel coding, and the encoder will send the parity bits in stages on the demands from feedback channel. Here, because fewer parity bits than the original are sent, the compression can be achieved in Slepian-Wolf codec. At decoder, "DWT LBS" block generates the referenced frames by low-band-shift (LBS) wavelet decomposing [33] for BMS.

From Fig. 5.17, the proposed scalable DVC framework has the following properties and advantages:

1. Complete intra-frame encoding model consists of intra-frame SPIHT and channel encoding, which makes our scheme have similar complexity as conventional intra-frame encoding.
2. There is no motion searching at encoder and just BMS is used at decoder. This avoids the prediction shift in conventional inter-frame encoding and brings more robustness than inter-frame encoding.

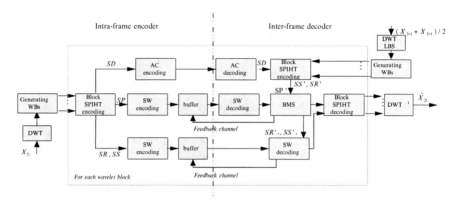

Fig. 5.17 The scalable DVC framework

3. The bit stream of block SPIHT of encoder can be received losslessly at decoder. It has embedded bit stream like conventional SPIHT.

From the above, the proposed framework preserves easy encoding and robustness. Additionally, the embedded SPIHT stream brings flexible bit points to be decoded. It is scalable in SNR property, but it can be extended to temporal and spatial scalability easily.

The following two sections will examine the proposed block SW-SPIHT and BMS with rate-adaptive "hash," respectively.

5.5.4   The Efficient Block SW-SPIHT

5.5.4.1   Block SPIHT

In the proposed system for Wyner-Ziv frames, their coding and motion searching is based on WBs. That is, a three-scale (it can be extended to more scales easily) DWT is implemented to Wyner-Ziv frames, and the resulting DWT coefficients are partitioned into 16×16 cross-scale WBs as in Fig. 5.18. In each WB, there are four 2×2 coefficients vectors from $LL^{(3)}$, $HL^{(3)}$, $LH^{(3)}$, and $HH^{(3)}$; three 4×4 from $HL^{(2)}$, $LH^{(2)}$, and $HH^{(2)}$; three 8×8 from $HL^{(1)}$, $LH^{(1)}$, and $HH^{(1)}$. Obviously, a WB is composed of several wavelet trees, so SPIHT can be used conveniently. This is the so-called block SPIHT. But note that all WBs use the same original threshold, the maximum value of the whole DWT image, in their block SPHIT. Experiment shows the block SPIHT has almost the same performance as conventional SPIHT for the whole image. This gives us base for block SPIHT combining Slepian-Wolf theory.

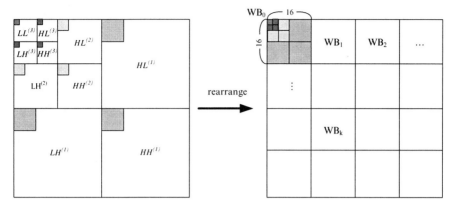

Fig. 5.18 To generate the WB

5.5.4.2 Block SW-SPIHT

Referring to Fig. 5.18, the block SW-SPIHT is described. At encoder, for a WB, after block SPIHT, we get the tree distribution information SD, significant information SP, sign information SS, and the refinement information SR. The distribution information SD is sent to the decoder by arithmetic coding. While, at decoder, the received SD is used to do block SPIHT for side WBs, and we get SP' and SS', and SR'. Then, SP', SS', and SR' are used to recover the main sequence SP, SS, and SR by lossless Slepian-Wolf decoding. This is the so-called block SW-SPIHT. Note that during the "block SPIHT encoding" at decoder, the distribution information SD of main WB is used to develop SP', SS', and SR' of the side WBs. This is different from "block SPIHT encoding" at encoder.

Here, we assume that the information of SPIHT is dependent if the WB, the wavelet tree, is similar.

But, maybe, the question which arises directly is which is the most similar WB. Based on the idea of wavelet domain motion searching in [33], the two WBs, at the same location or around the same location of main and side wavelet image, are similar. The WBs colocated at the no low-band-shift reference frame is referred to as the side information without motion searching. And the other selected WB is the one with motion searching as in the following sections.

5.5.5 BMS with Rate-Variable "Hash" at Decoder

Our contribution is also the BMS with rate-variable "hash" at decoder. The variable "hash" is based on SD and the partial parity bits of SP.

Here, what should be emphasized is that, in DVC, the motion searching is moved to decoder. But at decoder, there is no any information on current frame being encoded. So, in order to convey more information of current frame to decoder, we must send some efficient information to represent the current frame. This representation is just the function of "hash." In [13], the "hash" consists of a very coarsely subsampled and quantized version of the pixel block, and in [34], higher frequency coefficients of DCT act as "hash." But these "hash" are fixed rate. In the proposed work, we use SP as the helpful "hash." Since SP is the bit plane information of wavelet coefficients, relying on bit plane for the motion search still results in accurate motion estimation. Besides, in our scheme, because of the exploration of rate-adaptive SW-codec with feedback to SP, the hash bits are variable.

The concrete BMS with variable "hash" is explained as following. For a main WB with information SD, SP, SS, SR and the referred side WB with SP'_i, SS'_i, SR'_i,(where, $i \in (1, N)$ and N is the number of referred WB), the concrete searching is:

1. SW-encoding SP and storing all of its parity bits in buffer.
2. Sending the first part of parity bits of SP to decoder and judging if SP can be decoded correctly from SP'_1. If decoding succeeds the corresponding SS'_1, SR'_1 is used as SS'_s, SR'_s to decode SS and SR, otherwise $i = i + 1$ and try next referred WB.
3. Sending more part parity bit if SP cannot be decoded correctly by all referred WBs with fewer parity bits in step 2.
4. Repeating steps 2 and 3 until finding a side WB with the least parity bits sent for SP. And get the corresponding SS'_s, SR'_s.

5.5.6   Experimental Results

Similar to [31], only the luminance is tested for the first 101 frames of QCIF Carphone and 361 of Foreman with frame rate 30 Hz. The even frames are coded by Wyner-Ziv model as mentioned above, where, the SW-codec is based on accumulative LDPC [35]. The easy average interpolation of adjacent frame is taken as the side information assuming the odd frames are decoded completely. In the BMS, the region is $[dx, dy] = [-16, 16]$. Only the PSNR of the even frames are averaged, and the frame rate is 15 Hz. The experiments include:

1. Inter-frame coding performance of H.263+. (I-B-I-B)
2. Conventional SPIHT and the block SPIHT for even frames testing the efficient of block SPIHT
3. Block SW-SPIHT without BMS for odd frames testing the efficient of block SW-SPIHT.
4. Block SW-SPIHT with BMS showing the efficiency of motion searching

The results are shown in Fig. 5.19; from the results, we can see that the block SPIHT does not influence the performance of SPIHT. The SW-SPIHT can bring

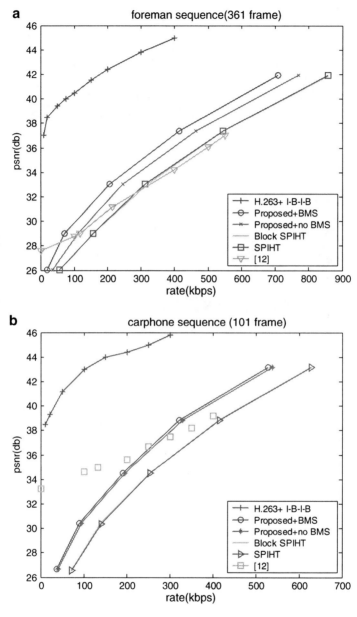

Fig. 5.19 The PSNR of scalable DVC framework. (**a**) Foreman.qcif, (**b**) Carphone.qcif

more than 2 dB improvement than SPIHT because the dependence is used at decoder. Also, the BMS at decoder gives more than 1 dB improvement for block SW-SPIHT, and the scalability is still preserved. But, for Carphone sequence, the motion searching is not so valid due to its motion being less.

Fig. 5.20 Original second frame (*left*) and decoded with 100% date (*right*)

Fig. 5.21 Scalable decoded Wyner-Ziv frame (*second frame*)

Additionally, our system has more than 2 dB improvement than Anne's pixel-domain DVC for Foreman sequence when only the easy average interpolation is used at decoder. This is because the DWT and SPIHT can abstract the dependence better at encoder. What is more, our scheme is scalable, and the truncated rate points are flexible like intra-frame SPIHT.

But, the proposed scalable DVC has lower SPNR in low bit rate because in the reconstruction, we only use the intra-frame decoding and do not use the side information. And our system has higher computation at decoding because of the motion searching, although it does not influence easy encoding.

Additionally, we give the original frame and decoded Wyner-Ziv frame with 100% rate in Fig. 5.20. The scalable decoded frames at different bits are shown in Fig. 5.21.

5.5.7   Summary

We have introduced a scalable DVC based on the embedded bit stream of block SPIHT. The scheme is easy, and the main property of DVC is preserved. Initial experiment results are encouraging, but much remains to be done. For example, the feedback in Slepian-Wolf coding makes the system invalid when there is no feedback channel. Maybe the similarity estimation should be done in future work. And for the robustness, the SPIHT is fragile to channel error; once a bit errs, the robustness loss is a lot. Maybe the multi-description coding (MD) is a better framework to protect the bit stream of SPIHT, and we will investigate the scalable DVC-based MD.

5.6 Robust DVC Based on Zero-Padding

5.6.1 Motivation

Robust DVC methods are necessary especially when video of low-power captures is transmitted over wireless network. DVC itself takes on inherent robustness because of the error-correcting channel decoding algorithm adopted. That is, Puri and Ramachandran [3] prove the robustness of DVC through experiments. But this robustness is achieved at the cost of compression efficiency. DVC assumes a correlation channel between the source to be encoded and its side information available at the decoder. In view of the principle of DVC, the compression efficiency comes from the correlation of side information, that is, more correlation means higher compression efficiency, and vice versa. While in the case of high packet-loss rate, the correlation of side information becomes low, so the compression efficiency is strongly limited. In some other works related to robustness, Wyner-Ziv video coding is used as forward error correction (FEC) to protect the video transmission. For example, Girod et al. [4, 36] provided a systematic lossy error protection (SLEP) based on Wyner-Ziv coding; the scheme is two-layer scalable in the sense of having one base layer with MPEG encoder and the corresponding Wyner-Ziv bits as the enhancement layer. However, SLEP scheme still applies motion estimation in its MPEG encoder, so the property of low-complexity encoding cannot be guaranteed to some degree. And, error propagation in the MPEG-encoded stream may negatively impact the quality of the side information and degrade the robustness of the system especially when the packet-loss rate is high. To improve the robustness of SLEP, O. Crave [37] addressed a distributed multiple description coding, while still, the high-complexity encoding was preserved due to the motion compensation temporal filtering at the encoder.

MDC has emerged as an attractive framework for robust transmission over unreliable channels. MDC encodes the source message into several bit streams (called descriptions) carrying different but correlated information, which then can be transmitted over the different channels. If some channels do not work, the lost descriptions can be estimated by the correlated descriptions received. MDC gives guarantee for robustness especially when the packet-loss rate is high due to its structure. Then, the robustness problem of DVC is addressed here by combining the multiple description coding. In this chapter, we attempt to design a robust multiple description DVC under the constraints of low-complexity encoding.

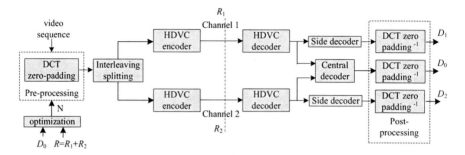

Fig. 5.22 Proposed framework of MDDVC

Recently, the multiple description (MD) version of pre-/post-processing is a popular technique for it does not require the modification to the source codec. It is proven that MDC with pre-/post-processing is much better than directly subsampling the original frames. For instance, in [38], the redundancy frames are added in the preprocessing based on the temporal correlation estimated by motion estimation. But the complexity of encoder is higher. In [39], redundancy is added firstly by padding various numbers of zeros in DCT domain to each frame. Especially, one-dimensional DCT zero-padding is attractive for it is an easy but efficient way. We attempt to design the robust MDDVC based on pre-/post-processing with simple 1-D DCT zero-padding scheme. Typically, the proposed scheme includes the following steps: first, in the preprocess stage, proper zeros are padded to each frame and a new sequence with big size is created. Next, MDDVC structures the sequence into two descriptions with each description compressed independently by HDVC algorithm of low-complexity encoding. At the decoder, the recovered video with good or acceptable quality is obtained by central or side decoder after post-processing stage. Here, note that the compressed HDVC descriptions are transmitted over different channels; when one channel does not work, the lost HDVC description can be estimated by those received from other channels, so the robustness is guaranteed even in the case of high packet-loss rate. Meanwhile, the proposed MDDVC avoids the complex motion estimation, and its encoding computation is similar to the intra-frame coding; thus, it has low-complexity encoding. In addition, thankfully, Fan Y. H. et al. [40] and Wu M. et al. [41] have done some beneficial work for MDC based on Slepian-Wolf to achieve better robustness. But still, there is much work to be done in robust DVC combining MDC under the constraint of low-complexity encoding.

5.6.2 Overview

Figure 5.22 illustrates our proposed scheme for MDDVC. In the preprocessing stage, the original video sequence is preprocessed to generate a new big-size video

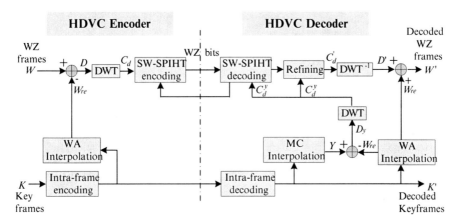

Fig. 5.23 HDVC framework used in the MDDVC

sequence using optimized 1-D DCT zero-padding [42]. And then by means of interleaving-splitting, the new sequence is divided into two descriptions, which can be compressed by any DVC scheme. Here, a proposed hybrid DVC (HDVC) scheme is employed for its efficient compression performance and low-complexity encoding. At the decoder, firstly, the central decoder merges the two decoded descriptions in case of no loss, or the side decoder uses error concealment method to estimate the lost description and create the concealed big-size video in loss case, and then in the post-processing, the inversed 1-D DCT zero-padding is implemented to recover the pixels. The details of HDVC, preprocessing, and post-processing are shown in the following two sections, respectively.

5.6.3 Hybrid DVC

To each description, an independent DVC codec is used to its big-size sequence. In view of low-complexity encoding and high rate-distortion performance, a new HDVC codec combining residual DVC [18] and Slepian-Wolf set partition in hierarchical trees (SW-SPIHT) algorithm [32] is proposed. The codec including HDVC encoder and decoder is shown in Fig. 5.23.

5.6.3.1 HDVC Encoder

In each description, the frames are classified as the key frames and Wyner-Ziv frames according to the coding method adopted. To the key frames, the intra-frame encoding of H.264/AVC is used. While to the other frames, the Wyner-Ziv ones, the following processes are implemented. Firstly, the weighted average (WA) interpolation is implemented to generate the referenced frame W_{re}:

$$W_{re} = \alpha K'_j + \beta K'_{j+1} \tag{5.11}$$

where K'_j and K_{j+1}' are the previous and next decoded key frames; $\alpha = 1 - l/g, \beta = 1 - \alpha$, where l is the distance between current frame and the previous key frame in the same group of picture (GOP), which has g frames totally.

Secondly, for each Wyner-Ziv frame W, the residual frame $D = W - W_{re}$ is decomposed by discrete wavelet transform (DWT), and the wavelet coefficient C_d is encoded by SW-SPIHT encoder. SW-SPIHT means that Slepian-Wolf codec is used to compress the SPIHT information of C_d, including the wavelet tree distribution information, the significant information, the sign information, and the refinement information. The details of SW-SPIHT can be seen in [43], where it is noted as "SPIHT with SI." The output of SW-SPIHT encoder forming the so-called Wyner-Ziv bits is sent to the decoder. The rate-adaptive low-density parity-coding accumulation (LDPCA) [26] with feedback is used for Slepian-Wolf codec. LDPCA with 396 nodes is adopted in our work. In the case of the sequence length less than 396, the padding-zero is applied.

Here, the encoding of HDVC mainly consists of DWT with SPIHT, LDPCA encoding, etc., which means that the complexity is similar to the intra-frame encoding so the low-complexity encoding is preserved. But note that the simultaneous exploitation of temporal and spatial correlations by the residual coding and DWT with SPIHT helps HDVC achieve better rate-distortion performance than DCT-domain DVC, which can be seen in the experimental results in Sect. 5.6.5. In addition, SPIHT-based HDVC can be easily extended to the scalable system.

5.6.3.2 HDVC Decoder

In HDVC decoding, the key frames are recovered by the intra-frame H.264/AVC decoder. While to the Wyner-Ziv ones, the following processes are implemented. Firstly, the decoded key frames are used to generate high-quality side information based on the bidirectional motion compensation interpolation as in Formula 5.12.

$$\begin{aligned}
Y(x, y) = \; & \alpha \times K'_j(x + \beta \times dx_f, y + \beta d y_f) \\
& + \beta \times K'_{j+1}(x - \alpha \times d_f, y - \alpha \times d y_f) \\
& + \alpha \times K'_j(x - \beta \times d x_b, y - \beta \times d y_b) \\
& + \beta \times K'_{j+1}(x + \alpha \times d x_b, y + \alpha \times d y_b)
\end{aligned} \tag{5.12}$$

where (x, y) are the coordinates of the interpolated frame, $[dx_b, d y_b]$ and $[dx_f, d y_f]$ are the backward and forward motion vectors between the decoded key frames, respectively, which may be obtained by the half-pixel motion estimation similar to [21]; α, β, and l are similar to that in Formula 5.11.

Fig. 5.24 To illustrate (**a**) 1-D DCT zero-padding and (**b**) its reversed process

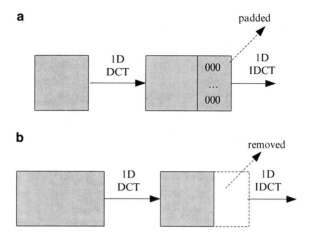

Secondly, DWT is implemented to the difference $D_y = Y - W_{re}$, and the resulting coefficient C_d^y is used as the side information for SW-SPIHT decoding. The refinement module is to recover the wavelet coefficients with the side information

$$C_d' = \{V_{max}, \text{ if } C_d^y > V_{max}; \quad C_d^y, \text{ if } C_d^y \in (V_{min}, V_{max}); \quad V_{min}, \text{ if } C_d^y < V_{min}\}$$
$$(5.13)$$

5.6.4   Pre-/Post-processing with Optimized Zero-Padding

MDC with pre-/post-processing is much better than directly subsampling the original frames. Especially, pre-/post-processing with DCT zero-padding technique based on the theory of zero-padding which shows padding zeros in frequency domain will result in the interpolation in time domain [39]. The interpolated frame is easy to be compressed because the correlation between pixels becomes strong, although it increases the frame size to be coded [39]. The concrete process of pre-/post-processing with DCT zero-padding is shown in the following. *Preprocessing*: one-dimensional DCT zero-padding, which has lower complexity and better rate-performance than two-dimensional DCT zero-padding, is illustrated in Fig. 5.24. Firstly, each frame is transformed using one-dimensional DCT on each row and then padded with zeros horizontally. After one-dimensional IDCT on new-sized row, we obtain the enlarged frame which is subsampled into two subframes by interleaving and independently coded by HDVC codec explained above.

Post-processing: After MDDVC central decoder or side decoder, two decoded subframes are obtained. Then, the two subframes are merged to get the big-size frames. Next, the inversed one-dimensional DCT padding illustrated in Fig. 5.24b is implemented to recover the original pixels, that is, the big-size frame is firstly transformed using one-dimensional DCT on each row, then padded zeros are removed, and IDCT is implemented to get the frame needed.

Optimized zero-padding: In the MDDVC with zero-padding, the number of zero-padded will affect the correlation as well as the rate-distortion performance of side and central decoder. Generally, when more zeros are padded, correlation between two descriptions will be higher producing better estimation and better quality from side decoder, while the central quality drops with the increasing of zeros. That is, more zero-padding benefits the compression in two aspects, one is that the lost description is estimated accurately, and the other is that the frames can be compressed easily due to the increased correlation between adjacent pixels. While on the other hand, more zero-padding makes the size of frame increase, which maybe requires more bits to represent it, and also, when no loss happens, more zero-padding means more redundancy added, so the central quality decreases. The aforementioned analysis requires an optimization for the number of zeros padded.

Let $D_0(f, N)$ and $D_1(f, N)$ (or $D_2(f, N)$) denote the mean squared errors (MSE) from the central and side decoder for the input image f, respectively, given the number of zero-padded is N. Let $R(f, N)$ be the bit rate for two descriptions, while $R_1(f, N)$ and $R_2(f, N)$ be the bit rates for the two balanced description 1 and 2, respectively. Our goal is to find the optimal parameter N in solving the following optimization problem:

$$\min_{N} D_1(f, N) \tag{5.14}$$

subject to

$$\text{condition1}: R(f, N) = 2R_1(f, N) = 2R_2(f, N) \leq R_{\text{budget}} \tag{5.15}$$

$$\text{condition2}: D_0(f, N) \leq D_{\text{budget}} \tag{5.16}$$

where R_{budget} is the available total bit rate to encode two descriptions and D_{budget} is the maximum distortion acceptable for central decoder reconstruction. The encoding optimization module in Fig. 5.22 is based on the above function. With the constraint on the total bit rate and the central distortion, N is adjusted accordingly to minimize the side distortion.

The optimization for the problem is carried out in an iterative way. The basic algorithm shown in Fig. 5.25 is to make use of the monotonicity of R and D as the function of N. After initialization, a smallest N is searched to minimize D_1 subject to condition 1 and condition 2.

5.6.5   Experimental Results

Here, there are mainly three groups of experiments taken into account to present the efficiency of MDDVC proposed. They are performance comparison of different coding methods, performance comparison with optimized zero-padding, and

Fig. 5.25 Zero-padding
optimization process

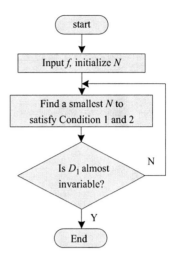

robustness comparison over packet-loss channel. In all of these experiments, the luminance components of standard sequences *Foreman* and *Hall* in QCIF@15 fps (frame per second) are tested. The total bit rate of two channels is accounted.

5.6.5.1 Comparison of Different DVC Methods

The performance of single description DVC (SD DVC) used will affect the performance of MDDVC proposed, so firstly, we compare our proposed SD HDVC with other SD DVCs referenced, including DVC of [21] and residual DVC of [18]. The GOP varies in 2, 4, and 8 to show the performance comparison.

Comparison curves in Fig. 5.26 shows that the proposed SD HDVC obtains up to 3 dB improvement for *Hall* sequence. There is even up to 3.9 dB improvement more than residual DVC in [18]. These improvements originate from the fact that the hybrid scheme can make use of some temporal and spatial correlations simultaneously at the encoder. For *Foreman* sequence, the improvement can also be achieved, although it is not as valuable as the *Hall* sequence due to the low temporal correlation.

Then, we plot the performance of the proposed MDDVC in Figs. 5.27 and 5.28, where the MD channels are assumed to be ideal, in which one channel is either intact or totally lost, that is, the information loss rate is 0% or 50%. The results show that the number of zeros added will affect the results of MDDVC, and even show that more zeros padded are not always helpful for the side decoder of MDDVC, such as in *Hall* sequence with 176 zeros. So an optimized zero-padding is necessary for introducing the proper number of zeros in the preprocessing stage.

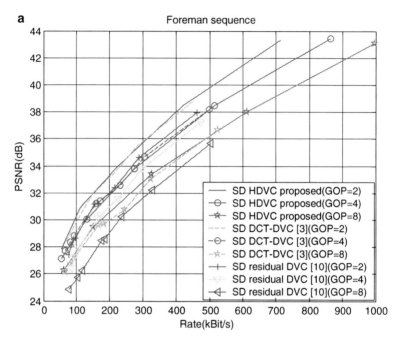

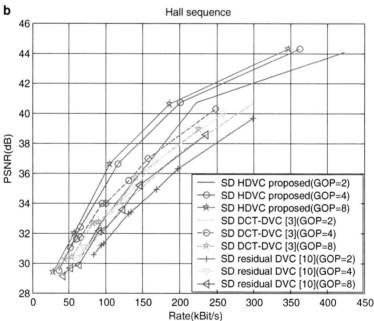

Fig. 5.26 Comparison of different SD DVC

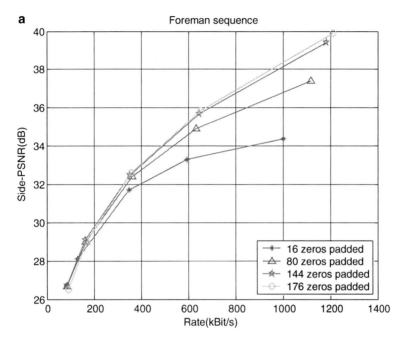

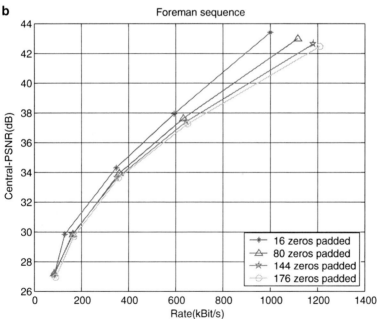

Fig. 5.27 Performance of different zero-padding for *Foreman* sequence

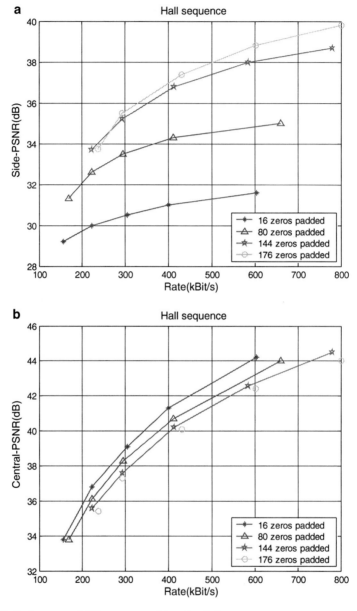

Fig. 5.28 Performance of different zero-padding for *Hall* sequence

5.6.5.2   Comparison of Optimized Zero-Padding

This experiment is to test the efficiency of the optimized zero-padding in MDDVC proposed. The comparison is based on the fact that the difference between the central

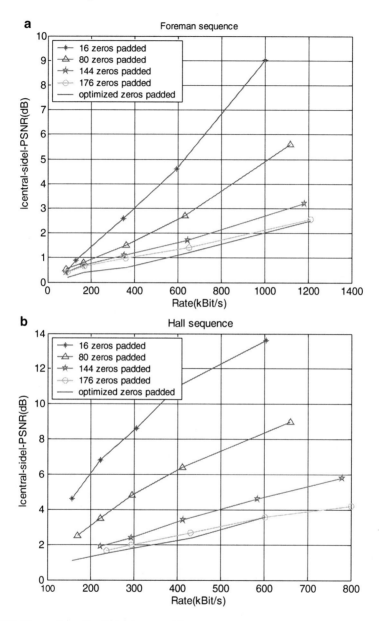

Fig. 5.29 Comparison of optimized zero-padding

and side quality illustrates the optimization performance of MDDVC when the same central quality and same bit rate are constrained during changing the number of zeros padded, that is, the smaller the difference is, the better the optimization is, and vice versa.

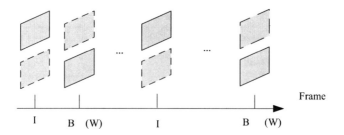

Fig. 5.30 Packet loss pattern

The optimization is implemented to each frame with the searching range variable from 0 to 176 zeros padded. The performance comparison is shown in Fig. 5.29. Obviously, the optimized zero-padding achieves the smallest difference between the central and side quality due to its trade-off consideration of side and central quality. And it also shows that less zeros should be padded in the case of low bit rate.

5.6.5.3   Robustness Comparison over Packet-Loss Channel

The two above experiments test the performance when half of the information is lost, while in practice, the loss is not so serious, so this experiment will divide the frames into packets and test the performance when partial packets are lost.

This experiment compares two methods: proposed MDDVC method and SLEP based on [4] but with H.264 and SW-SPIHT codec instead of the MPEG and SW-DCT. In case of SLEP, each frame is divided into two subframes by interleaving, and each subframe is compressed and packed independently. The packet loss pattern is shown in Fig. 5.30, which assumes that the two subframes in the same frame are not lost simultaneously. At the decoder, the lost subframes are estimated by average interpolation, and then the estimated values are corrected by the SW-SPIHT bit stream. In the case of MDDVC, it is just each big-size frame that is divided into two subframes and packed independently. While, the packet loss pattern is the same as that of SLEP mentioned above. GOP is set to 2, 4, and 8 for SLEP with "I-B-B-B" order and for HDVC with "K-W-W-W."

Figure 5.31 shows the results of reconstruction quality with different packet-loss rate when total bit rate is 1,100 kBit/s for *Foreman* and 610 kBit/s for *Hall*. It is clear that our scheme has evidently better robustness than SLEP when loss rate is high. However, unlike SLEP, MDDVC does not perform better with the increasing of GOP especially for the high motion sequence *Foreman*. This is because the side information becomes bad in big GOP, which affects the performance of SDDVC and MDDVC, while noting that SLEP performs good when the GOP value is big at the cost of the increasing of encoding computation.

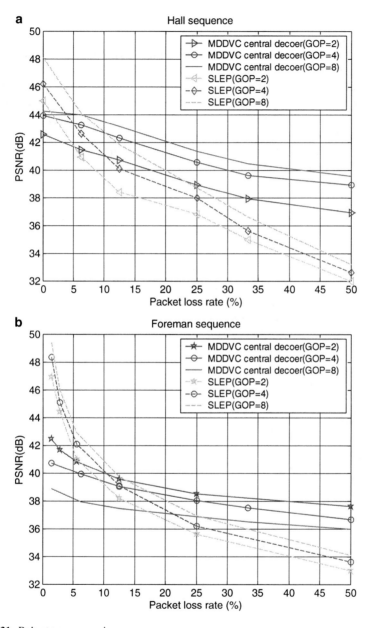

Fig. 5.31 Robustness comparison

5.6.6 Summary

A new robust MDDVC scheme combining the distributed video coding (DVC) and multiple description coding (MDC) is proposed. The encoding of MDDVC mainly consists of one-dimensional DCT zero-padding, DWT, SPIHT, and LDPCA encoding, etc. Thus, the proposed scheme avoids the complex motion estimation and preserves the low-complexity encoding similar to the intra-frame coding. MDDVC guarantees its robustness in view of structure, that is, when one channel does not work, the lost HDVC description is efficiently estimated by the received from other channel. The proposed scheme is promising in the video communications of low-power devices over network, such as wireless sensor network, mobile camera, and so on.

References

1. Slepian, D., Wolf, J.K.: Noiseless coding of correlated information sources. IEEE Trans. Inf. Theory **19**, 471–480 (1973)
2. Wyner, A., Ziv, J.: The Rate-distortion Function for source coding with side information at the decorder. IEEE Trans. Inf. Theory **22**(1), 1–10 (1976)
3. Puri, R., Ramchandran, K.: PRISM: an uplink-friendly multimedia coding paradigm. In: Proceedings of International Conference on Acoustics, Speech, and Signal Processing, Hong Kong, pp. 856–859 (2003)
4. Griod, B., Aaron, A., Rane, S.: Distributed video coding. Proc. IEEE **93**(1), 71–83 (2005)
5. Rebollo-Monedero, D., Aaron, A., Griod, B.: Transform for high-rate distributed source coding. In: Proceedings of Asilomar Conference Signals, Systems and Computers, Pacific Grove (2003)
6. Wang, A., Zhao, Y., Hao, W.: LVQ based distributed video coding with LDPC in pixel domain. In: Lecture Notes in Computer Science in Artificial Intelligence-9th Pacific Rim International Conference on Artificial Intelligence, (PRICAI 2006), Guilin, pp. 1248–1252 (2006)
7. Conway, J.H., Sloane, N.J.A.: Fast quantizing and decoding algorithms for lattice quantizers and codes. IEEE Trans. Inf. Theory **IT-28**(2), 227–232 (1982)
8. Servetto, S.D.: Lattice quantization with side information. In: Proceedings of IEEE Data Compression Conference, Snowbird, pp. 510–519 (Mar 2000)
9. Liu, Z., Xiong, Z.: Slepian-Wolf Coded Nested Quantization (SWC-NQ) for Wyner-Ziv coding: performance analysis and code design. In: Proceedings of Data Compression Conference, Snowbird (Mar 2004)
10. Aaron, A., Rane, S., Griod, B.: Toward practical Wyner-ziv coding of video. In: Proceedings of IEEE International Conference on Image Proceeding, Barcelona (2003)
11. Aaron, A., Rane, S., Setton, E., Griod, B.: Transform-domain Wyner-Ziv codec for video. In: Proceedings of Visual Communications and Image Processing, VCIP-2004, San Jose (Jan 2004)
12. Ascenso, J., Beites, C., Pereira, F.: Motion compensate refinement for low complexity pixel based on distributed video coding. http://www.img.lx.it.pt/~fp/artigos/AVSS_final.pdf
13. Aaron, A., Rane, S., Griod, B.: Wyner-Ziv video coding with hash-based motion compensation at the receiver. In: Proceedings of IEEE International Conference on Image Processing, Singapore (2004)
14. Wu, S.-W., Gersho, A.: Joint estimation of forward and backward motion vector for interpolative prediction of video. IEEE Trans Image Process **3**(5), 684–687 (1994)

15. Rowitch, D.N., Milstein, L.B.: On the performance of hybrid FEC/ARQ system using rate compatible punctured turbo codes. IEEE Trans. Commun. **48**(6), 948–959 (2000)
16. Wang, A., Zhao, Y., Wei, L.: Wavelet-domain distributed video coding with motion-compensated refinement. In: Proceedings of IEEE International Conference on Image Processing (ICIP'06), Atlanta (2006)
17. Martinian, E., Vetro, A., Ascenso, J., Khisti, A., Malioutov, D.: Hybrid distributed video coding using SCA codes. In: Proceedings of IEEE 8th Workshop on Multimedia Signal Processing, Canada, pp. 258–261 (2006)
18. Aaron, A., Varodayan, D., Girod, B.: Wyner-Ziv residual coding of video. In: Proceedings of Picture Coding Symposium, Beijing, pp. 28–32 (2006)
19. Wang, A., Zhao, Y., Pan, J.-S.: Residual distributed video coding based on LQR-hash. Chin. J. Electron. **18**(1), 109–112 (2009)
20. Wang, A., Zhao, Y., Pan, J.S.: Multiple description image coding based on DSC and pixel interleaving. In: Proceedings of International Conference on Intelligent Information Hiding and Multimedia Signal Processing, Harbin, pp. 1356–1359 (2008)
21. Artigas, X., Ascenso, J., Dalai, M., Klomp, S., Kubasov, D., Ouaret, M.: The DISCOVER codec: architecture, techniques and evaluation. In: Proceedings of Picture Coding Symposium, Lisbon (Nov 2007)
22. Girod, B., Aaron, A., Rane, S., Rebollo-Monedero, D.: Distributed video coding. Proc. IEEE (Special Issue on Video Coding and Delivery) **93**(1), 71–83 (2005)
23. Tagliasacchi, M., Trapanese, A., Tubaro, S., Ascenso, J., Brites, C., Pereira, F.: Intra mode decision based on spatio-temporal cues in pixel domain Wyner-Ziv video coding. In: Proceedings of IEEE Conference on Acoustics, Speech, and Signal Processing, Toulouse (May 2006)
24. Tsai, D., Lee, C., Lie, W.: Dynamic key block decision with spatio-temporal analysis for Wyner-Ziv video coding. In: Proceedings of IEEE International Conference on Image Processing, San Antonia (Sept 2007)
25. Wang, A., Zhao, Y., Pan, J.-S.: An efficient hybrid distributed video coding. IEICE Electron. Express **5**(17), 650–656 (2008)
26. Varodayan, D., Aaron, A., Girod, B.: Rate-adaptive distributed source coding using low-density parity-check codes. In: Proceedings of Asilomar Conference on Signals, Systems and Computers, Pacific Grove (Nov 2005)
27. Wang, A., Zhao, Y., Zhu, Z., Wang, H.: Scalable distributed video coding based on block SW-SPIHT. Chin. Opt. Lett. **5**(6), 336–339 (2007)
28. Xu, Q., Stankovic, V., Xiong, Z.: Layered Wyner-Ziv video coding for transmission over unreliable channels. Signal Process. (Special Issue on Distributed Source Coding) **86**(11), 3212–3225 (2006)
29. Sehgal, A., Jagmohan, A., Ahuja, N.: Scalable video coding using Wyner-Ziv codes. In: Proceedings of Picture Coding Symposium. San Francisco, CA, Dev (2004)
30. Tagliasacchi, M., Majumdar, A., Ramchandran, K.: A distributed-source-coding based robust spatio-temporal scalable. In: Proceedings of Picture Coding Symposium. San Francisco, CA, Dev (2004)
31. Aaron, A., Zhang, R., Griod, B.: Wyner-Ziv coding of motion video. In: Proceedings of Asilomar Conference on Signals and Systems, Pacific Grove (2002)
32. Tang, C., Cheung, N., Ortega, A., Raghavendra, C.: Efficient inter-band prediction and wavelet based compression for hyperspectral imagery: a distributed source coding approach. In: Proceedings of IEEE Data Compression Conference, Snowbird (Mar 2005)
33. Park, H., Kim, H.: Motion estimation using low-band-shift method for wavelet-based moving-picture coding. IEEE Trans Image Process **9**(4), 577–587 (2000)
34. Aaron, A., Girod, B.: Wyner-Ziv video coding with low encoder complexity. In: Proceedings of IEEE International Conference on Image Processing, San Francisco (2004)
35. Varodayan, D., Aaron, A., Girod, B.: Rate-adaptive distributed source coding using low-density parity-check codes. In: Proceedings of Asilomar Conference on Signals, Systems, and Computers, 2005, Pacific Grove (Nov 2005)

36. Rane S., Aaron A., Girod, B.: Systematic lossy forward error protection for error-resilient digital video broadcasting-a Wyner-Ziv coding approach. In: Proceedings of International Conference on Image Processing, Singapore, pp. 609–612 (2004)
37. Ascenso, J., Beites, C., Pereira, F.: Motion compensate refinement for low complexity pixel based on distributed video coding. In: Proceedings of International Conference on Advanced Video and Signal-Based Surveillance, Como, Italy (2005)
38. Bai, H., Zhao, Y., Zhu, C.: Multiple description video coding using adaptive temporal subsampling. In: Proceedings of International Conference on Multimedia Exploring, Beijing, pp. 1331–1334 (2007)
39. Wang, D., Canagarajah, N., Redmill, D., et al.: Multiple description video coding based on zero padding. In: Proceedings of International Symposium on Circuits and Systems, Vancouver, pp. 205–208 (2004)
40. Fan, Y.H., Wang, J., Sun, J., et al.: A novel multiple description video codec based on Slepian-Wolf coding. In: Proceedings of IEEE Data Compression Conference pp. 515 (2008)
41. Wu. M., Vetro. A., Chen. C.W.: Multiple description image coding with distributed source coding and side information. In: Proceedings of SPIE Multimedia System and Application VII, pp. 3–10 (2004)
42. Wang, A., Zhao, Y., Bai, H.: Robust multiple description distributed video coding using optimized zero-padding. Sci. Chin. Ser. F Inf. Sci. Inf. Sci. 52(2), 206–214 (2009)
43. Wang, A., Zhao, Y.: Efficient wavelet zero-tree video coding based on Wyner-Ziv coding and lattice vector quantization. In: Proceedings of International Conference on Innovative Computing, Information and Control, Beijing, pp. 245–258 (2006)

Chapter 6
DVC-Based Mobile Communication System

6.1 System Framework

As mentioned in the former chapters, we can see that the most important characteristic of DVC is its low-complexity encoding, which is especially suitable for the low energy consumption of video communication equipment. In this chapter, we will build the DVC system to realize video communication over wireless network. This system is also constructed as the platform for the DVC algorithms mentioned above, which has been supported by the National 863 Project of China.

Figure 6.1 is the framework of DVC-based mobile communication system, where two low-power smartphones can be connected to the campus network via the Hot Spot. Here, the communication from *A* to *B* can be taken as an example, shown in Fig. 6.1. After the establishment of the communication network, smartphone *A* will transfer the DVC stream into the base station through the Hot Spot. Then at the base station, the received DVC stream will be transformed into H.264 coding stream, which will be transmitted over the campus network and finally reach the smartphone *B*. Similarly, we can use the same way to transfer the DVC stream from *B* to *A*, thus realizing the video communication between two smartphones.

6.2 Development Environment

6.2.1 Hardware Environment

In this system, we use the hardware equipment as follows:

1. Two smartphones. Here, a smartphone of HTC Xda Atom Life in Fig. 6.2 is chosen as the smartphone *A* and a smartphone of Dopod CHT9000 in Fig. 6.3 as the smartphone *B*. Both of them adopt Windows Mobile operating system.

H. Bai et al., *Distributed Multiple Description Coding*,
DOI 10.1007/978-1-4471-2248-7_6, © Springer-Verlag London Limited 2011

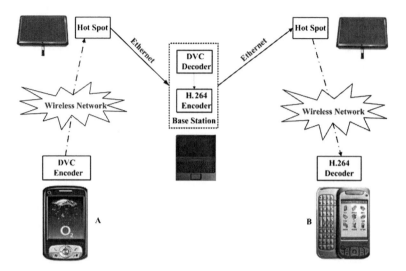

Fig. 6.1 Framework of DVC-based mobile communication system

Fig. 6.2 HTC Xda atom life

Fig. 6.3 Dopod CHT9000

2. One personal computer (PC). It can be regarded as the base station. Windows XP Professional XP2 operating system is installed in it.
3. Campus network. Here, we use campus network to build the network environment.

6.2.2 Software Environment

Based on Pocket PC Phone operating system of Windows Mobile, we developed this system. Windows Mobile operating system is derived from the classic Microsoft Windows operating system, which leads to similar user interface to some extent. Windows Mobile operating system has powerful functions, such as audio/video player, surfing on the Internet, MSN chatting, and e-mail. Most smartphones which support Windows Mobile operating system use Intel-embedded processor, which results in high clock speed. Additionally, smartphone equipped with this operating system has better performance than those equipped with other operating systems in some hardware equipment such as RAM and memory card. However, this series of mobile phones also has some disadvantages. For example, as a result of high configuration and more functions, the power consumption may be great, and the battery duration is always short. Therefore, the low-complexity encoding and decoding algorithm is significant. Pocket PC Phone provides operating system for the one-handed operation smartphone. It is the most popular Microsoft smartphone operating system. A majority of Microsoft operating system–based smartphones on the current market adopt this operating system, such as Lenovo ET180, ET560, DOPOD696, and CU298. Pocket PC Phone operating system completes most operations with the help of stylus.

The development software includes Visual Studio 2005 [1], Microsoft SDKs, and Windows Mobile 5.0 Pocket PC SDK [2]. Figure 6.4 is the user interface of Visual Studio 2005, and Fig. 6.5 is the device emulator of Pocket PC SDK.

6.2.3 Network Environment

Two smartphones are connected to the campus network through the WiFi, while the PC for base station is linked to the campus LAN by the general network cable. Thus, communication can be constructed among the three devices. WiFi is a kind of IEEE 802.11 wireless network protocol, namely 802.11× [3]. Its highest bandwidth is 11 Mbps, but when the signal is weak or disturbed, the bandwidth can be adjusted to 5.5, 2, and 1 Mbps, which can guarantee the stability and reliability of the network effectively. The main feature of WiFi is its fast speed and high reliability. In the open area, the communication distance can reach 305 m, while in the closed area, the communication distance ranges from 76 to 122 m. Therefore, it is convenient to integrate with the existing Ethernet, and network integration is at lower costs.

Fig. 6.4 Microsoft visual studio 2005

Fig. 6.5 Pocket PC emulator

Because of the characteristics mentioned above, we used WiFi in our system for the wireless communication.

To implement network communication, we selected the Client/Server model based on TCP/IP and the connection-oriented stream socket. Here, PC in base station can be regarded as server and two smartphones as clients. The communication principle is as follows: First, both the server and client must establish

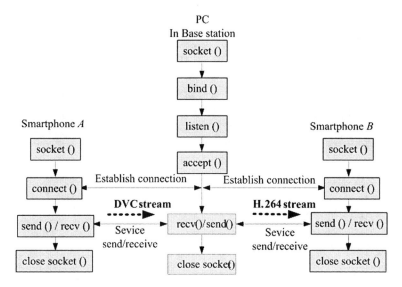

Fig. 6.6 Client/server communication process

communication socket, and the server is in the listening state. Then, smartphone *A* may use socket to send connection request to the server. When the server receives the request from *A*, it will establish another socket to communicate with *A*, and the former socket is still responsible for listening. When another client, smartphone *B*, sends connection request, the server will establish a socket again to communicate with *B*.

According to the framework in Fig. 6.1, we design client/server communication process for DVC-based mobile communication system as shown in Fig. 6.6. At the beginning of communication, both the client and server will call the function of socket () in Windows Sockets API to establish sockets. Second, the server can call the function of bind () to bind the socket with a local network address. Then, the server will call the function of listen () to make itself in a passive state for receiving and set the length of request queue. Lastly, the server can receive client connection by calling the function of accept ().

Compared with the server, the work of the client is quite simple. When the client opens a socket, it can establish a connection with the server through the function of connect (). After the connection establishment, the data can be sent and received between client and server. For example, smartphone *A* sends DVC streaming to the server, while smartphone *B* receives H.264 streaming from the server.

Finally, when the data transmission is over, PC in base station and client will call the function of closesocket () to close a socket to complete the communication.

Fig. 6.7 Experiments on pixel domain

6.3 Experimental Results

The experiments of DVC are performed on pixel domain, according to the basic principles illustrated in Chap. 5. Here, we no longer assume that the odd frames can be transferred to the decoder without distortion, but use the H.264 intra-coding to compress odd frames. Additionally, removing the feedback channel, a fixed number of check bits will be sent according to the reconstruction of WZ frames in base station. Since at the decoder the algorithm of motion compensation interpolation is adopted to produce side information, the decoding sequence of video frames is different from the encoding, that is, the encoding order is processed frame by frame 1-2-3-4-5-6-7-..., while the decoding order is 1-3-2-5-4-7-6-....

Two smartphones are chosen as the clients, as shown in Fig. 6.7. Smartphone A adopts HTC mobile phone as shown in Fig. 6.2, and smartphone B adopts Dopod mobile phone as shown in Fig. 6.3. It is noted that smartphone A displays the captured video, and the base station PC displays the video after DVC decoding, while smartphone B displays the video finally reconstructed by H.264 decoding. We can see that the quality of the recovered video is fine, as shown in Fig. 6.7. Figure 6.8 further shows the visual quality of the two smartphones. In Fig. 6.8, the left smartphone is used to capture the video, and after wireless network transmission, we can get the recovered video sequence from the right smartphone. It can be seen that our DVC-based mobile communication system not only receives high-quality recovered video but also realizes the real-time video transmission

6.4 Summary

In this chapter, the development environment of DVC-based mobile communication system is briefly introduced. Further, the establishment of WiFi communication is explained in detail. Experimental results depict that the proposed system realizes the video communication between two low-power mobile phones with satisfactory quality.

Fig. 6.8 The captured and recovered video

References

1. http://msdn.microsoft.com/en-us/library/ms950416.aspx. Accessed on October 29, 2011
2. www.microsoft.com/downloads. Accessed on October 29, 2011
3. Gast, M.: 802.11 Wireless Networks: The Definitive Guide. O'Reilly Media Inc., Sebastopol, CA (2005)

Index

H. Bai et al., *Distributed Multiple Description Coding*, DOI 10.1007/978-1-4471-2248-7,   173
© Springer-Verlag London Limited 2011

CPSIA information can be obtained at www.ICGtesting.com
Printed in the USA
LVOW090230150212

268752LV00004B/20/P